MIKE RO WAVE

DR FLUKE

CAL PAL

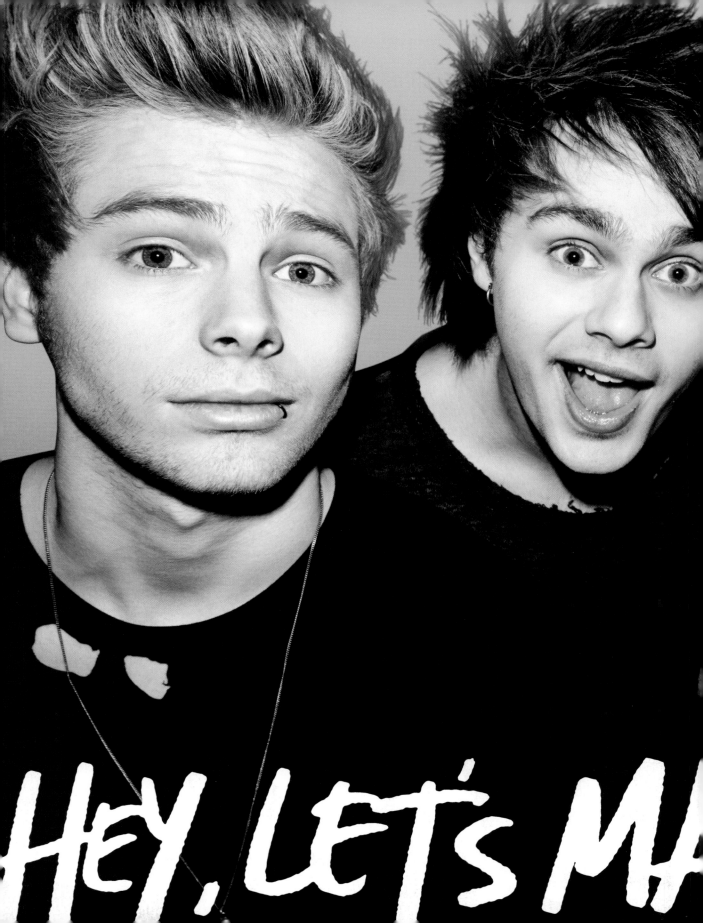

HEY, LET'S MA

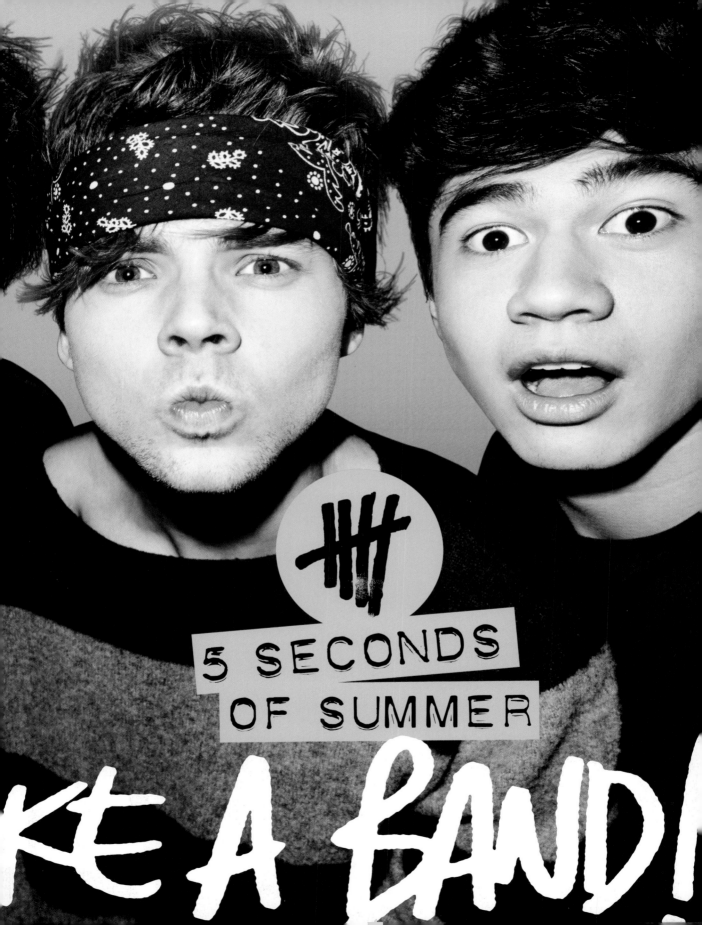

Library of Congress catalog card number: 2014949037
ISBN 978-0-06-236644-3 (trade bdg.)

14 15 16 17 18   LP/RRDR   10 9 8 7 6 5 4
❖
First Edition

5 Seconds of Summer assert the moral right to be identified as the authors
of this work

All band photography courtesy of Liz Hemmings with the exception of
pp 2-3, 6, 15, 22-3, 28, 43, 56, 76-7, 95, 138-9, 151, 160, 174, 213, 288, back endpaper
© Tom van Schelven

Illustrations and doodles on cover, front endpaper, pp 21, 44, 101, 218 by
Rich Andrews; cartoon strip on pp 142-145 by Chris Rowland

All textures and background images © shutterstock.com

THANK YOU!

This book wouldn't have been possible without our amazing fans,
who have got us where we are today. The ones who stand for
hours on end to watch us play, the ones who would support us
four dudes through thick and thin. You are our everything.

Thanks also to Matt Allen.

COnTeNTS

UcTION

What you're about to read is pretty much
our story so far. It really does seem like
only last week we played our first gig at
the Annandale Hotel in Sydney. Since then
we've been given the opportunity to turn
into the people and musicians we wanted to be.
The people who gave us the opportunity were
the fans. The ones who stand for hours on end
to watch us play, the ones who would support
us four dudes through thick and thin.
Everything goes back to the fans.
You guys are our everything.

So this book is like a thank-you. We want
everyone to know the story of how four
Western Sydney teenagers picked up their
instruments and dreamed of being one of the
biggest bands in the world. There's also some
embarrassing photos of us derping around
and some facts that we didn't even know.
So we hope you enjoy it!

Love cal, luke, ash, and mike x

Sent from my iPhone

HEY, LET'S

PaRT 1:

MAKE A

BAND!

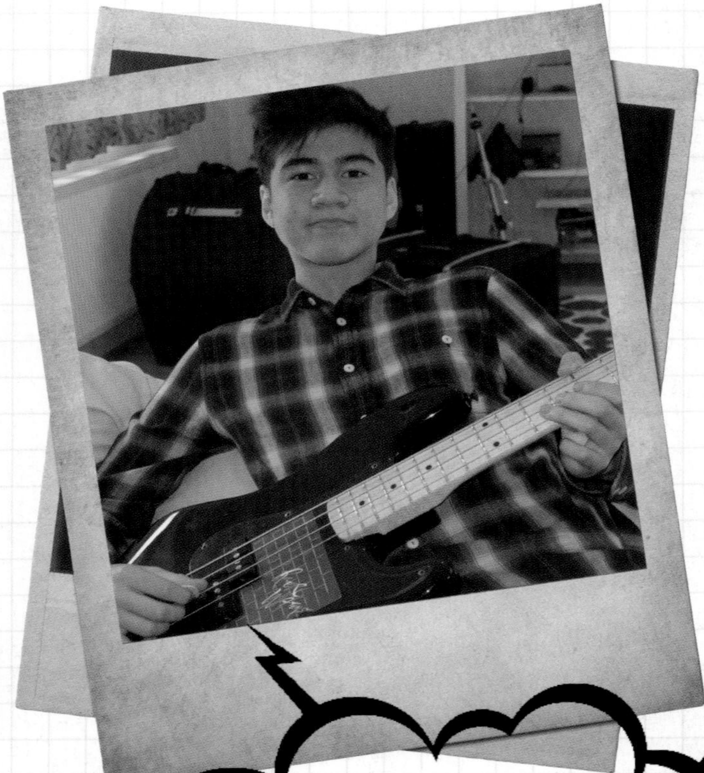

CALuM

TORN IN TWO

How 5SOS came to be is a pretty crazy story ...

When we started the band, the dream was to get guitars back on the radio because that's the music we grew up with. The love of rock and punk music brought Michael, Luke, Ashton, and me together when we were at school, but when I was younger my life could have gone one of two ways. I really loved football and I wanted to become professional. My favorite team was Liverpool and I dreamed of walking alongside their captain, Steven Gerrard. But as soon as I discovered music I knew it was the only thing I wanted to do.

I was always the "sporty" one in my family. When we were at school, my older sister, Mali, was the musical one. I used to listen to her sing at school and at home and wonder why I was never as talented or as good as her at music. I definitely gained a lot of my love of music from her; she would blast R&B out of her bedroom.

We were a middle-class family. Mum worked in superannuation and Dad had a job with Coca-Cola, so it wasn't the most glamorous life. Mum and Dad weren't very musical but they could both sing. I remember my dad singing along to The Proclaimers out the back and not being able to get to sleep because of it. But I was extremely grateful – my parents gave me everything I needed with what little we had.

I was a shy kid at school. I never really spoke to anyone I didn't know or make too much eye contact. It took me a while to come out of my shell, sort of – joining the band helped a lot. Despite my shyness back then, though, I made friends at school, but there were only a few close ones that knew a lot about me.

The only real classes I liked were PE and Music. I loved anything to do with sport. PE was always great and I'd like to think that I was good at English, but Music was kind of an escape. That was the class I looked forward to the most. In music I really felt myself. I always found time to play terribly on different instruments.

As a pupil, I think I was quite well behaved – but that changed a bit when I moved up into high school at Norwest and every single teacher's comment on every report card read: "Calum has potential, but he gets distracted too easily." That was my life summed up in a sentence. As I grew older my grades got worse and worse. No matter how hard I studied I just didn't excel. Later, there was a certain point when the band started where my grades went down the drain and my parents weren't happy at all. It's not cool to suck at school, but by then I didn't really care about anything other than the band.

HANGING WITH THE BAND

I first met Michael when I was in Year 3 at Norwest Primary. He had the best fringe I'd ever seen. But the one thing I remember about him as we got older was that he was really tall. He must have gone through puberty when he was 12. The beard kinda gave it away.

We really became friends a bit later, when we started at Norwest Christian College. We did music classes together and started playing guitar. I always used to love watching him play. He was so talented for his age.

When I was about 15 I saw a classical guitar lying around in my house. I had no idea whose it was but I picked it up. Although I really struggled at first, it didn't feel like a task to learn to play it. For months on end I'd come home from school and look up videos on YouTube on how to play; I used to always play in front of my parents

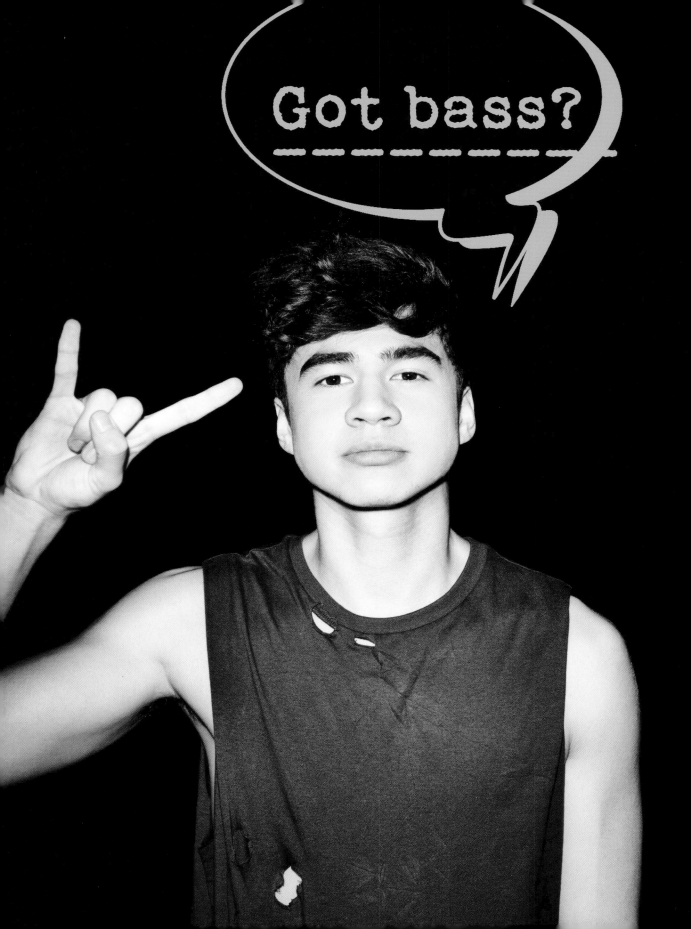

and they used to love it – they kind of had to, they were my parents. When I was 16 they bought me my first steel string for my birthday and I used to take it to school all the time, but back then I never would've thought I'd pick up the bass.

I was 13 when I first met Luke. He joined our school in Year 7 and because he had an older brother, he'd made some older friends. I always wished I had that. I can still see him now, wearing a green jumper with one of those snapback hats with a peak at the front. I didn't look so great either. I wore really short shorts and my legs were so skinny. My head was shaved, too. I was in a bad place.

Because of my sister, I really liked R&B acts like Chris Brown, but I soon fell in love with the American pop–punk and punk–rock bands like Green Day, Blink-182, and The All-American Rejects. I instantly fell in love with the sound.

I remember the day when music took over my life: I was on the bus on the way to school and my sister's friend's brother handed me a burned CD with "Green Day – *American Idiot*" written on it in permanent marker. I put it in my CD player and literally could not stop listening to it. I loved everything about it: the angst, the rawness, the distorted guitars; it almost took me out of reality. I loved the energy and the emotion in all the parts; there was power in the songs. Every time I heard the opening chords of the album *American Idiot*, it always made me wonder how they wrote the album. I learned how to play their song "Good Riddance" and when I strummed it to some cousins on my new guitar they said, "Hey, you should play more often...."

Michael and I always liked the same kind of music – bands like Blink-182, All Time Low, and Green Day are the reason why we each picked up an instrument. That was unusual in our school because there weren't a lot of kids

like us around. If you were really into music like we were it was thought of as being a bit weird, and a lot of the other students looked at us like we were outsiders.

Then Michael and I started sitting together in music classes and playing songs. There was an event every year called Live At Norwest where all the kids that could perform something would get up and play in front of the whole school. Because we got on and liked the same bands, the pair of us decided we would play "Beauty in the Breakdown" by a band called The Scene Aesthetic. I would love to say that it sounded good, but it didn't. Luke played that night as well – he played Jason Mraz. He also had a broken wrist! He was crazy at guitar. I knew how much he practiced. He used to put up covers on YouTube. I thought he was amazing.

At first I thought Luke didn't hang out with me because he hung around with an older crowd, but I went up to him and said how much I loved his stuff on YouTube. We became friends after that and the next time Live At Norwest came around, me and Luke did a song together. At first Michael, Luke, and I never played together – it was always Luke and me, or Michael and me – but once Michael asked Luke to play I also wedged my way in.

Luke, Michael, and I then started to hang around in the music room, jamming and playing riffs. We were there for as long as we were allowed, which was good for me because by the time I'd got to being 14 or 15, I'd found that school was tough. I'd got into Norwest on a sports scholarship, which meant I had to play sports all the time. At first I loved it, but once I discovered music, I realized that's all I wanted to do. Football fell away – I wanted to spend all my time playing with the guys.

Then, one afternoon in December 2011, Michael said those words: "Wanna start a band?"

HEY, LET'S MAKE A BAND!

DR FLUKE

LUKE

IN MY OWN LITTLE WORLD

It's funny, I can't remember what I did yesterday most
of the time, so I struggle to remember my childhood, but
my mum always tells a story from when I was really little.
Apparently, she came into the kitchen and caught me
with my hand in a tub of margarine. I was eating the
stuff off my fingers, which must have tasted awful, not
that I seemed to care at the time.

I was a happy kid. We lived in a small town called
Freeman's Reach and I came from a small family – just me,
Mum, Dad, and my two older brothers, Ben and Jack.
Mum was an accountant, then she became a math teacher.
In fact, she taught Ashton for a year or two. She always
said he wasn't the best student, but that he was a really
nice person.

Although we weren't a massively musical family, my
dad liked all the older Australian bands like INXS and
AC/DC, so there was always music being played when I
was little. Mum had played the piano, though there was
never one around the house, but it was Ben and Jack who
started me on playing the guitar. Ben had tried to learn
when he was younger, and there was an electric lying
about that I would pick up and play. Jack had a
drum kit in his room, so sometimes we would make
a noise together.

The first song Ben taught me was Deep Purple's
"Smoke on the Water," when I was 10, and I would play
it on the top string with one finger. I did it so much that
there was a massive crease in the skin and I think I must
have driven everyone crazy, playing that same song all
the time. Later, I learned the lyrics to Green Day's

"Holiday," and for some reason, I would sit in my room singing it over and over until my dad would come in and shout at me to stop.

I wasn't a bad kid, but I was always getting into trouble for stupid things. At primary school I was in a world of my own and often I would get told off for being too loud. Then when I was around six, I wouldn't go to class. I would be in school, but running around the playground having a great time while everyone else was in lessons. The teacher would look around at the students" faces and, having realized that I wasn't where I was supposed to be, she would race into the playground shouting, "Come here, Luke! You're going into detention!" When you were really naughty you'd have to sit on a chair outside the principal's office. It was terrifying.

I think I was quite smart in primary school. My grades weren't too bad, but most of the report cards would be like, "Luke would benefit from not sitting with his friends." That was my own fault, and I guess I liked talking too much. When it came to subjects, I wasn't so good at English, and I was terrible at drawing and art. Math was my subject, though. Well, Mum was an accountant and a math teacher, so I felt I had to be good at that.

I was sporty, too. I played football when I was a kid and my team was Manchester United, so I loved watching Wayne Rooney and Cristiano Ronaldo play. I was also a pretty good swimmer. I'd win all the races at my school and I would compete against other schools in regional competitions. But it wasn't long before music was taking over my life.

CURTAIN OPENED, HEARD THE CROWD ROAR

By the time I'd got to Norwest Christian College, my high school, I had really long hair and a fringe that went over my face. I joined in Year 7 but didn't know anyone else because a lot of the kids had gone to Norwest's primary school together, so I was really nervous at first. It's always tough when you turn up somewhere and you don't recognize a friendly face. I guess to everyone else I was the weird guy with the long hair, so it was a pretty lonely time. I didn't have that many friends until Year 9, and I spent a lot of lunchtimes on my own in the music room.

With high school it was the same story as primary school. I kept getting into trouble for small-time stuff — being stupid in class, spending too long on my phone, getting distracted. Sometimes I'd even get told off for not wearing the right uniform. At Norwest you would get demerit points whenever you broke the rules, and if you scored five points you had to go to an after-school detention. I think I was in one of those every few weeks.

Having learned some guitar riffs from Jack, I later took some proper lessons and I would even sit in my room watching tutorials on YouTube. I was becoming completely obsessed with learning how to play. I also loved noisy guitar bands like Foo Fighters and Good Charlotte, so it was natural that I would get to talking to Calum and Michael in school because they were the other outsiders at Norwest and loved those bands as well. The energy and loud guitars of punk made sense to me and the three of us became pretty close once we started going to the same music lessons.

It's funny, Michael and I didn't like one another when we first met a couple of years earlier in Year 7, when I first joined the school. I don't know what it was — I didn't really talk to him. It was probably because he was taller than me and he looked more like a man. I'd hang out with Calum a little bit, but I don't think Michael liked that either, because they were friends. Then, in Year 9, Calum and I covered a song by the band Secondhand Serenade at the school talent show, Live At Norwest. Maybe there was a bit of rivalry with me and Michael because previously he had performed with Calum, I don't know.

That show was so nerve-racking because we had to play in front of the whole school and our voices hadn't even broken then. That was an awful experience. I'd much rather play in front of 20,000 people than perform in front of the school — all the people that you know and have to live with every day. Still, we got plenty of applause, which felt great, but it was probably only because everyone had to clap. I don't think the girls went mad, though. We weren't too popular where we grew up when it came to girls. I was learning that at our school it was much better to be good at sport than be into music. The jocks were the popular kids; punks like us seemed a little odd to everyone.

Just before Live At Norwest, I had taken the step of recording videos of myself as I covered songs by artists like Bruno Mars and Jason Mraz in my room at home. I'd posted them on YouTube because that was the thing at the time — loads of new songwriters were doing it, so I figured I'd give it a go too. I was 14 and had no idea what I was doing, but suddenly I was getting a few thousand views for each one and people at school were

THE 5 FACTS YOU NEED TO KNOW ABOUT 5SOS

#1

We nearly called ourselves Bromance (that was Luke and Cal's idea) until we all decided it was lame.

#2

On one of our early tours, a sinkhole swallowed the club where we were due to be playing. We didn't want to disappoint the fans who'd bought tickets, so we shifted our gear to a nearby school and rocked out on the tennis court.

#3

When we were recording our debut album in LA, a group of fans sent a gang of male strippers to our front door! We thought we were getting burgled!

#4

When we were writing "She Looks So Perfect," Michael wasn't keen. It took him a while to get into the song.

#5

We wanna be a band for many years to come and grow with our fans!

saying nice things about them. I would chat to people who had been listening to my music, but despite the attention, I was oblivious to what it all meant.

It was shortly afterwards that Michael came up to me. I think he'd seen the songs online and had realized that I liked the same sort of music as him. After the ice was broken, we would hang out in music class, jamming, talking about all the bands we loved until one day he came up with the idea that the three of us should start our own band — something like All Time Low or Blink-182. He figured it would be interesting if we put some songs onto YouTube. I liked the sound of that. Being in a band, hanging out with friends, and writing songs sounded so exciting. But I had no idea of what was coming next.

HEY, LET'S MAKE A BAND!

MICHAEL

SITTING HERE AT HOME

Wow, looking back I was such a nerd when I was a kid.
Most of the time I was stuck in front of a computer screen;
because Mum and Dad owned a computer business, they
had all the gear, and some of my earliest memories are
of playing games at home. I loved it, but luckily for
me it was my gateway into 5SOS.

When I was little, my dad played drums, which is
where I must have got all my rhythm from. But when I was
around eight or nine, my parents bought me the video
game *Guitar Hero*. Once I started playing I got
ridiculously good at it. So good that I thought, *Hey!
Maybe I should try playing guitar for real ...*

Until that point, I hadn't really shown any musical
talent. We grew up in a place called Quaker's Hill, which
was a pretty OK town – it had a Domino's Pizza place
and a McDonald's, which was great as I got older, but as
a kid it was pretty dull. I was mainly sat in front of a
computer screen and there's even a picture of me, aged
about two, playing on a keyboard. I became quite an
intense nerd. It's a miracle I didn't end up turning into
some kind of mad scientist.

I think that became a problem, because I hated
school. I never wanted to go to lessons and often I refused
to leave the house. I remember my parents being really
angry at me because I wouldn't go in, even when I was
at primary school. I don't know what it was, but there was
something I absolutely hated about the lessons. They
sucked. Now we're in the band and getting up and

working hard, I'll me. Back men, school was like torture to me.

It wasn't like I couldn't do the subjects, though. I went to Norwest Primary, the same as Calum, and then on to Norwest Christian College, the high school. When I was really young, maybe in Year 3, I was placed in the gifted and talented class. I was smart. I was good at English, was awful at math, but I understood everything and I could get what the teacher was saying. Still, I hated it.

kept thinking, *Why the hell am I in a class that needs me to be smarter when I don't even want to be here in the first place?* Everyone else was so dedicated to school. They were getting all these amazing grades and I was like, "Forget this." The next year they put me in the average class.

When I was about 12 or 13, life got a bit tougher for me because the recession happened and it hit Mum and Dad really hard. I was an only child and until then I'd been pretty spoiled, I guess. I hadn't realized what money was worth because I was so young. I would just ask for things and get them, no problem. Once I'd got into my teenage years and my parents went broke, it made me realize that I couldn't expect everything to happen for me.

Now I'm in the band, I appreciate absolutely everything we do together. Every time we're on stage, I'm happy. Every time we're meeting fans or signing autographs for people, I make sure I enjoy it, because know from my parents how hard life can be when things aren't running so smoothly. Even when I'm tired from all the shows and touring, I tell myself how lucky I am. got all of that from my childhood. That was a pretty important lesson to pick up.

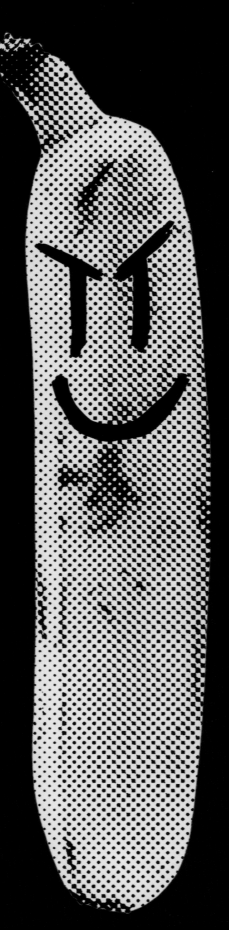

LET'S GET OUT

Getting into *Guitar Hero* made me fall in love with punk, metal, and old-school rock. I loved playing along to songs by bands like the British metal band DragonForce and also Metallica because on *The Black Album* they delivered riffs that were so damn heavy they blew my head off.

I'd play that game over and over – I even got a *Guitar Hero* drum kit. I always thought that shredding it on *Guitar Hero* – that's when you play loads of notes, super fast – was more impressive than shredding it on a real guitar.

When it came to playing the real thing, oh dude, it was so hard! At first I tried singing lessons, but I hated them. Then I tried playing the piano. Eventually, when I was 11, Mum and Dad bought me a crappy acoustic guitar from a shop down the road, but when I started taking lessons, I nearly quit straightaway. I was like, "No way, this is so tough." My guitar teacher, David, kept encouraging me and I eventually got over my frustrations of not being able to play anything. Now I'm in our band I'm so glad I stuck with it. Imagine if I'd given up and never picked up the guitar again?

The first song I learned from start to finish was that awful tune "Ode to Joy" – you probably would have heard it at school. After that I got to play Led Zeppelin's "Stairway to Heaven," but really badly. Then came the basic rock classics, like Deep Purple's "Smoke on the Water." I drove everyone mad playing that, but it soon paid off and after a year of practicing, I got an electric guitar when I was 11 years old. It felt cool to bash out songs really loud on the amp.

MICHAEL:

We have a song called "Everything I Didn't Say." I love the sentiment of a song that's about the things you could have said to someone. I also really like the line from "Good Girls": "Good girls are bad girls that haven't been caught." I think that's badass.

WHAt's FavoriTE

LUKE:

"Take me back to the middle of nowhere," which is from "Long Way Home." Half of the album was written by Michael, Ashton, or Calum and I like the songs they've written. They're by my band, but I'm further away from those lyrics because I didn't write them. I think I like those tracks more. And that's a really cool lyric.

CALUM:

There's a song on the album called "Never Be" with the lyric, "We'll never be as young as we are now." I think it's really cool. We wrote that as a band with John Feldmann in LA. But the funny thing is, we were all writing it from different perspectives, which means that people can listen to that song and interpret it in different ways. Like the song says, I don't feel I'm getting older. I still feel really young. It's like I'm 16, and I'm just waiting for that rugged stage to happen where I get facial hair.

YOUR SOS LYrIC?

ASHTON:

I'm like Calum, I love the line from "Never Be": "We'll never be as young as we are now." That song's all about how we're doing what we do at the moment and that, right now, people want to listen to our music. Me and the boys are between 18 and 20, and we're living in the moment. It won't be like this forever. I want to grab it. I hope people see that in us — that we're growing up.

I was getting into some great bands back then. *Guitar Hero* tuned me in to some of the older rock groups like Led Zeppelin, which then directed me to Blink-182 and Green Day.

But it was the American band All Time Low that got me really excited. I loved their songs. They mixed pop and punk so perfectly and they looked like they were having a great time, all the time. Alex Gaskarth, their lead singer, had such a powerful voice, which worked so well with some seriously infectious guitar hooks. I was sold on them straightaway. He was an absolute dude, too. I wanted to be in a band because of them; I guess I started singing because of Alex as well – he was a hero to me at that time.

Up until Year 7 I was an absolute geek. I'd had a few friends, other geeks, but other people at school didn't really like me that much. Then I manned up a little: I got myself a girlfriend and I met Luke in a Year 7 orientation day at Norwest. I also became friends with Calum. We had known each other since Year 3, but we hadn't really hung out that much. It wasn't long before we were all really close.

It was music that brought us together, because, I admit it, when I first met Luke I figured, "He's too cool. He's the type of guy I can't be friends with." He thought he was great (but he wasn't!). But Calum was really nice, he was the guy who everyone liked. I guess I was the guy who everyone didn't. I also looked a little bit different to everyone else. I wanted to dress like Lil Wayne, but at the same time I wanted to look like Alex Gaskarth. I was kinda confused.

There was also a period, just before we'd hit it off, where Luke and I hated one another for a bit. It was over a girl at school. He'd really liked her and I'd liked her,

too, but I'd asked the question first. For a while Luke was always being rude to me, but once we started talking music together, we got over it. But Luke was cool. I knew he was really into his music because he had been making cover versions of songs by people like Jason Mraz and posting them on YouTube. They were OK – not great – but there was something interesting about them.

Suddenly, Luke, Calum, and I spent all our time together, hanging out in Music class. When we weren't in lessons, we were in the music room playing riffs together. All of us had guitars, so we would learn songs and mess around. When it came to the school's annual show, Live At Norwest, Luke and Calum did a song together. I went on my own and did a medley of songs by the band Panic! At the Disco. I really liked it, but I only got a 7/10 score. Still, in my head it was amazing.

Then one day in school, I turned around to the others and said, "Dude, what if we started a band like All Time Low?" I thought it would be great if we could hang out and make real songs together; playing our guitars as loud as we could and writing records as iconic and vital as *American Idiot* or All Time Low's *Nothing Personal*. They got excited and said, "Yeah, man, why not? It would be awesome." And the rest is history.

ASHTON

I'VE GONE FROM PLACE TO PLACE

One of the things I can tell you about growing up in Australia was that I never stayed in one place for too long. My dad left when I was two, and me and Mum moved around a bit, from home to home – sometimes we even lived in caravan parks. At times I had to meet new friends and get used to new homes, which was pretty tough.

Most of the time, we were in a place called Windsor, which was about an hour and a half out of Sydney. When I started at primary school, I was a good kid, but I used to get into trouble with the teachers loads because I was very loud. Every report card said the same thing: "Ashton gets distracted a lot. He should concentrate more." I guess I just wanted to be funny and I loved being the center of attention.

Luckily I was pretty smart, otherwise I would have been in some serious trouble with Mum. She was kinda strict when it came to schoolwork and if I played up, or didn't do well in classes, she wouldn't stand for it. She could be pretty frightening sometimes, but I knew she was only doing it because she loved me and wanted what's best for me.

Living with her was great, though; she encouraged me to do so many things away from school – stuff she thought would improve me as a person. I played football, which I loved, and I did acting classes. The one thing I was really good at was swimming, but it was hard work. As I got older and the training became more serious I used to swim seven days a week. I'd finish school in the afternoon and

then walk to training. I'd come home really tired and then I'd have to get up early the next day to go swimming again. It was intense. Now the smell of chlorine makes me sick.

I tried to be good at everything I did when I was in primary school – that was my attitude. It's the same now: whenever I go out and play a show with the band, I want to raise the bar, I want everyone to come away thinking, *That's a great band,* or, *That dude's a great drummer.* Back then, I wanted to be the best at all the classes. Except for Math – I was absolutely awful when it came to numbers. English was pretty cool because I enjoyed writing stories. Later, when I went to high school, I loved Science. I thought it was fun because I could blow things up, cut cows' eyeballs open, and do other weird stuff.

At times it was hard for me and Mum because we were on our own. We didn't have a lot of money and we'd struggle to eat from week to week at times. But that became a normal thing to me. I'd go to a friend's house and they'd say, "What do you want for dinner?" I'd tell them, "Oh I'm fine, I don't want to intrude." I was used to living on a budget but that was my whole childhood. We did what we could to get by.

MIXTAPE '94

One of my earliest musical memories happened when I was around seven or eight. I used to have a tape recorder and I would sit in my room and wait for my favorite songs to come on the radio. Then as soon as I heard a riff I liked or recognized, I would press "Record" and tape the track, and at the end of the day I'd have a whole album full of stuff. It's funny, we have a lyric on our single "She Looks So Perfect" that goes, "I made a mixtape straight out of '94." That line was inspired by those days.

HEY, LET'S MAKE A BAND!

I guess my musical education really started when Mum met her boyfriend, Warwick. He was a drummer in a local band and he loved music. They were always listening to albums together, and I remember at the time it used to really annoy me because they would play music so late at night. It was always bands like Counting Crows and Smashing Pumpkins, and the guitars would be blaring out of the lounge, but it was nice because they were in love. The sight of them staying up and listening to music together is a really cool memory for me.

Those times also taught me a lot about different bands and developed my taste in music. My musical tastes were a little bit different from a lot of kids' at school, I guess. I didn't go to the same place as the other guys, and when I started at Richmond High School I was really into pop–punk bands like Green Day, Blink-182, and The Living End – stuff I'd discovered when I was making my mixtapes. Green Day quickly became my favorite band ever. I loved their energy and the songwriting.

I think the first song of theirs that blew me away was called "Jesus of Suburbia." I used to love their singer, Billie Joe Armstrong, and I would play a Green Day live album called *Bullet in a Bible* all the time. I listened to it so much that I knew the words off by heart – even the parts where Billie Joe would talk to the crowd. They were definitely the band I wanted to be in when I was growing up.

When I was around nine, a friend of mine called Lachlan asked me if I wanted to be in a band with him. He was a guitar dude and he had a drum kit at his house. I figured, "Yeah, I want to be in a band, just like Green Day!" The only problem was, I hadn't learned to play any instruments at that time – but that didn't stop me! I told Lachlan that I could play the drums and he seemed pretty happy to have me come around to his house to play.

When my mum dropped me off and I got inside, I sat behind the kit and tried to play a song called "The Mexican Hat Dance," but it was so bad. Lachlan looked at me funny. He was like, "You can't really play drums, can you?" I tried to laugh it off. "Yeah, I can," I said. "I'm just not very good today."

Luckily for me, Warwick was a drummer. I remember seeing him later that day and saying, "Hey, can you teach me something? Next week I'm going back to Lachlan's and I want him to think I can play." As soon as he gave me a lesson, I picked it up really quick. I fell in love with the drums after that. I couldn't get enough – that's all I did from that moment.

When I got to high school, the swimming started to be too hard for me. I was competing in regional events, and I even reached state level, but by the time I was 14, I couldn't stand it. I didn't get to hang out with my friends or play the drums as much as I liked, so I told my mum that I didn't want to swim anymore. It was devastating for her, but I'd had enough. I hated it.

As I got better on the drums, I got my first step up. Warwick let me play with his band. They would do shows every Saturday and I would come on at the end of their concert and play a song or two, something like Red Hot Chili Peppers' "Dani California," or "Sweet Home Alabama" by Lynyrd Skynyrd. Most kids would hang out with their friends on the weekend, but to me, hanging out with Warwick's band and playing to 40 people at a show was the best thing ever. Think about it: a kid playing drums with his mum's boyfriend's band in a pub? Seemed pretty punk to me.

BRAND

PART 2:

NEW
WORLD

A DAy TO rEMEMBeR

LUKE:

I'll never forget our first ever recording session. It was in 2011 and Michael, Calum, and I came together in the music room at school one lunchtime. We decided to do a cover of a song called "I Miss You" by Blink-182. They were a band we really loved and we'd jammed the song a few times, so we knew how to play it through. Calum and I were on acoustic guitars and we all sang, though what was funny was that we were reading the lyrics off our phones. We'd looked the words up online and downloaded them rather than taking the time to learn the songs off by heart.

We were just winging it at that time, I guess. Back then, the thing to do if you were in a band was to record a cover and put it on YouTube. Loads of artists had started that way, and I already had my channel, so the three of us figured we should put our version of "I Miss You" up there, just to see what happened.

Later on we did a cover of "Teenage Dirtbag" with Ash. We all went to Michael's house, where he had a garage. We could record and jam in there because his parents were cool with it, so we stuck up a video camera and recorded ourselves playing. It was pretty DIY.

At the time we thought "I Miss You" was pretty cool. Looking back it was kinda lame, but it still feels pretty crazy that once we'd put it online people actually watched it.

CALUM:

We were wondering what the hell was going on. I guess we must have been kinda naive because we kept putting up these really bad covers online – and we knew they were bad, but we were like, "Forget it. Let's just do it anyway." In our minds we were having fun, we weren't taking it very seriously.

We picked the songs we thought people would like. I guess we put these up because where we came from, music wasn't really the coolest thing to do. You were a lot more popular if you were into sports, playing rugby or Aussie rules. People at home didn't really care about what we were doing – they thought we were freaks, outsiders – so we were hoping for some recognition elsewhere. We wanted to make something of ourselves.

None of us had any idea of what might happen. It wasn't like we were thinking of touring the world and playing shows to thousands of people. Our idea was, "Yeah, cool, let's keep putting up covers. You write some songs, I'll write some songs, and we'll come together and practice."

ASHTON:

I used to watch the boys on YouTube, and I knew about them in the local area. I was in a couple of other bands at the time and I was doing weird gigs with jazz bands and African drumming bands at school. Whenever I saw one of their covers, I'd think, "Man, they could be so much better!" They just mucked around a lot — they didn't seem that serious really.

I wasn't in the band at the time some of the early covers were recorded, and it's funny looking back at them, but those videos were definitely what got people interested in the band at the beginning. Cool thing was it spread internationally, not just in Australia. It was getting more views in Sweden than it was at home. I think that's really where it started to broaden out and the band became a little bit of a thing elsewhere. In the end, 600,000 people looked at that video. Six hundred thousand! That was insane.

BECOMING 5SOS

MICHAEL:

So, here's how we came to be called 5 Seconds of Summer: it all happened just before we'd started posting stuff online. The three of us were playing together and we were clearly a band, but we didn't have a name yet.

In my mind I wanted a name that was a bit like the All Time Low album *So Wrong, It's Right*. When that came out, their fans changed the name to suit them, so it would go, "So Wrong, It's ... Catherine" or, "So Wrong, It's ... Michael." I thought, *Wouldn't it be amazing if we had that, too?* At the time, we had no idea we would even get fans, it was all a bit of a fantasy.

At first I thought we should be called 5-Second Summer, but it didn't feel right, so I went for 5 Seconds of Summer, or 5SOS. The next day Calum, Luke, and I were sitting in Science class together and the teacher was talking about neutrons and protons or something. That's when I said to the others, "Listen, I think we should go with the name 5 Seconds of Summer."

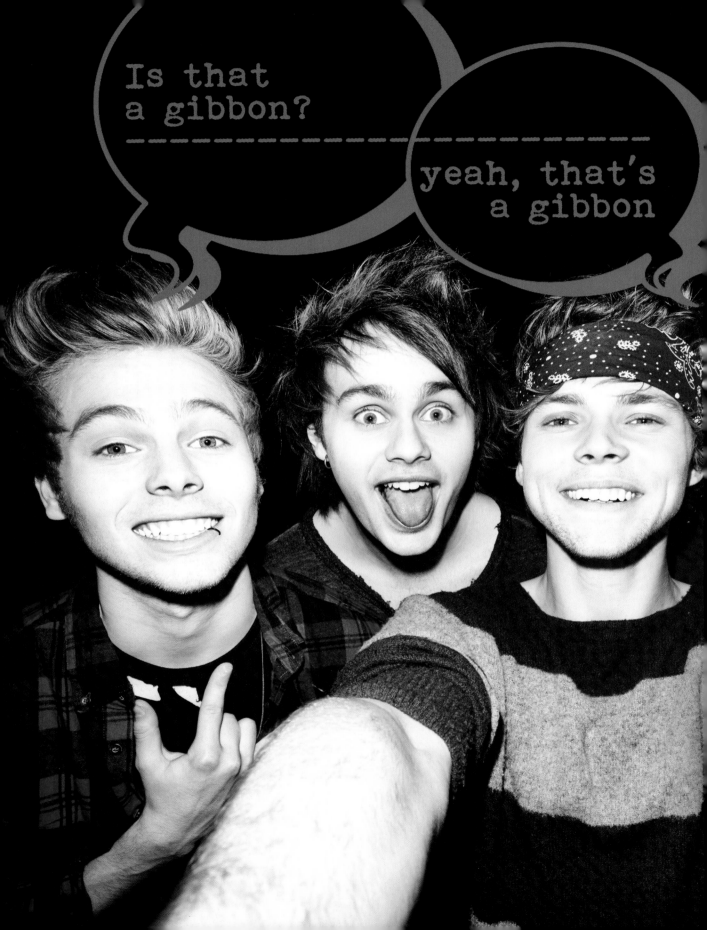

The class ended and I texted them later that day. I wrote, "Hey guys, I'm making the band 5 Seconds of Summer." (I think I still have that message on my phone actually.) Not long afterwards, I made the Facebook page, I made the Twitter page, and then we were up and running.

GO OUT ON A HIGH NOTE

LUKE:

When we came up with our first song, it was amazing.
Calum wrote it, and it was called "Gotta Get Out."
I remember thinking, *This is awesome!* It was great for the
time – it was a pop–punk tune, with a great guitar intro,
and it was better than anything I had written.

We didn't know that he could write that well. I don't
think Calum even knew that he could write that well – but
he could. He was coming up with really cool riffs and
tunes. I remember at that time we only had one mic stand
at Michael's house and one mic between us, so Calum and
I were having to switch every time we sang. It was so
basic, it was insane.

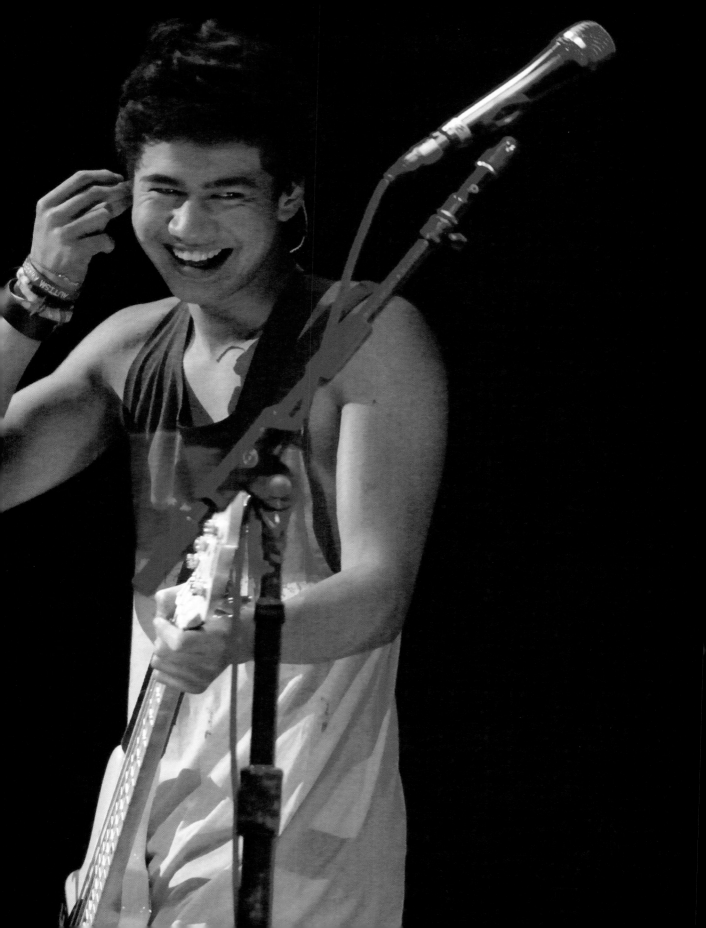

CALUM:

I found it quite easy to write songs and I would do everything on a rubbish little guitar in my bedroom. When I wrote my first ever song, I started with a few lines and then the rest of it came together in around two hours. It just came out of me. It was a new thing for me, so I guess I wasn't putting too much time into it. When I had finished the song I felt weird as s**t. A while later, I went into the music room with the other guys and played them "Gotta Get Out" and they seemed to like it a little bit.

The main thing for me was that it was cool knowing I could write songs – songs that meant something. I could never really express how I felt or put it into words, even to my family, so songwriting was how I expressed everything, and it was a massive deal for me. I pretty much fell in love with it.

MICHAEL:

When Calum came to us with "Gotta Get Out" I was amazed by the way it was so hooky. We've written better songs since then, but to start out and have that as our first track was pretty cool. I remember playing it on my acoustic guitar for my music teacher in class and he said, "Wow, if you guys keep having songs like that you're gonna be big."

A TICKET TO ANOTHER WORLD

MICHAEL:

This is going to sound crazy but, in December 2011, I somehow talked a guy who owned the Annandale Hotel pub in the city into giving us a gig. Our first show! It was ridiculous. The Annandale had a history. It was an iconic venue, kinda like the old 100 Club in London where the Sex Pistols played, or CBGBs in New York where punk started. Then when we announced it on our Facebook page, 300 people said they were going to turn up, even though we'd never done a show before.

That's when we came to the realization that we weren't prepared at all. We sat down and talked it out. I said, "So, guys, what are we going to do for the gig?" We didn't have a drummer, but because the three of us had been making music together we thought we'd just get someone in to help us for the night.

Then we went through the possibility that I could play drums and someone else could play bass. In the end I was like, "OK, we should stick to what we're good at, which is Calum on bass [even though he'd never played one before], Luke on guitar and me on guitar. That means we just need to find another person to play drums."

At first we asked this guy Matt, who came from school, to play drums for us, but he said, "No, I don't think I can

make it to the gig." Then I remembered this dude called Ashton who I'd met at a party. He was a friend of a friend and I knew he was a pretty good drummer, so I got onto Facebook and messaged him with a note saying: "Hey, man, I don't know if you know our band, 5 Seconds of Summer, but we're doing this gig in the city soon – do you wanna play?" He came back straightaway saying, "Yeah, man. I'd love to!"

CALUM:

I had a problem. At the time, my football was going really well and my family were keen on me playing. I used to train with a coach called Marshal, and around the time that 5SOS were getting together, he said to me, "Do you want to go training in Brazil? My friend runs a place over there." At first I wasn't sure. I knew that Brazil was a crazy football country and that they produced some amazing footballers over there, like Neymar, but I also knew it was a big step for me. Brazil was miles away, the other side of the world, and I'd barely traveled anywhere by that time in my life. I didn't know how I would handle being so far away from home.

Eventually, Marshal talked me into it and once I'd said bye to my parents, I was out there for a month. The whole experience was unreal – the people, the culture, the food – it was all incredible. I was staying about three hours out of São Paolo and I played a lot of football every day. It was pretty mental and so cool to be in Brazil, but after a while I did start to get a bit homesick. Communicating was pretty hard too, as nobody spoke much English. I love going to different countries and meeting different people, especially now with the band, but back then I was out there on my own and it did get a bit overwhelming.

Music was also taking over my life at that time, and I'd decided I wanted to do the band over football. Even though nothing had really happened and we'd only scored one gig, I kept thinking back to our last 5SOS rehearsal before I'd flown out of Australia. That day it felt as if we were on the verge of something exciting. Everyone was really excited about the gig, which was due to take place two days after I got back.

SMASH

HERE'S ASHTON

ASHTON:

It meant so much to me to be drumming in 5SOS that I
rode my bike for 10km to get to Michael's house for our
first practice. It was such a long way and it took me ages.
When I got there I was hot and sweaty, and I think the
other guys were a bit weirded out by it, but I didn't mind.
I was sick of messing around with bands that didn't care,
that didn't have larger-than-life ambitions. I just wanted
to make something of myself with music. I needed to find
some people who wanted to commit to a band and give
everything to it and give up everything for it and go
anywhere to do it.

When I got there, only Michael and Luke were around,
Calum was still in Brazil and, man, did I have questions.
"Do you have original songs? Are we doing any covers?"
But the others didn't seem to care. They were sitting there
playing video games. I was definitely no expert, but they
seemed so clueless about all the work they had to do to
be great at the gig and it really bugged me. Finally, after
an hour and a half, we went into the garage at Michael's
where there were guitars and an electronic drum kit.

Anyway, I listened to the songs and I loved them.
There was some great stuff there. I was like, "Wow,
they're really good." There was a song called "Gotta Get
Out" that was cool. There was another track called
"Conversations" and one called "Heartbreak for Two."

They were quite heavy, quite metal. And straightaway I thought, *These guys have got it, we could do something great here.* So I went home and I was really excited. I remember saying to Mum, "Wow, I've met the guys and they've got 12,000 followers on Twitter and we're doing a gig – you need to come ... Can you drive me in?"

LUKE:

Ashton was a great drummer – as soon as he started playing he seemed tight, he hit really hard. The only off-putting thing was the fact that he was wearing a horrific purple shirt and some three-quarter-length shorts, which looked a little weird. He was also sweating buckets because he'd ridden his bike all the way from his house, which was miles away.

After Ashton left, me and Michael got together and had a talk about what we thought. Michael was like, "He's cool, he's really good on the drums. We should get him in the band!" He was right. After that it was only a case of getting him to learn the songs. He was definitely the last piece of the puzzle.

MOVE TO THE BEAT

CALUM:

The month of 5SOS's first ever gig was an important time for me because I had to think about a lot of things. I got home and told my parents that I wanted to quit football and take the band more seriously. They weren't very happy and it was a pretty tough week in my life. Mum and Dad gave me everything to play football when I was a kid, so for me to say, "I don't want to do it anymore ..." well, that must have been a bit of a shock.

Looking back, that was a tough decision. I knew the chances of making it would be slim. It was difficult for my parents to handle because they'd encouraged me so much and supported me whenever I played, so I definitely understood how they felt.

I was so glad that I'd made that decision, though, because when I went to see the other guys they'd already tried out Ashton for the band. He was such a good drummer, but when I met him I was actually a bit intimidated because he was so big; he was older than me and a great musician, but he was cool. The third time I hung out with him I stayed over at his house and once Michael had left for the evening, I was like, "S**t, I'm by myself with this guy I hardly know." But we got on really well and we became great friends.

So with Ashton on drums and Michael and Luke on guitars, it was up to me to pick up the bass. In the final practice before our first gig, I used an acoustic guitar and just played the bass lines on the top string. The first time I actually played bass was when we got on stage at the Annandale Hotel.

I was like, "This is so cool!" But I was absolutely terrible at playing, I had no idea what to do. I soon fell in love with it, though. Afterwards I really got into bassists like Mike Dirnt from Green Day.

MICHAEL:

That first gig was so bad, though! When we got to the venue, the 300 people who said they were going to turn up didn't arrive and there were only 12 people there, plus our parents. But on stage it just felt really good to be able to play music. It felt right.

I don't even think we had a set list of songs that night. We played one or two of our own songs, like "Gotta Get Out," but we mainly played covers. We'd finish one song and then we'd shout out to the audience, "What do you want us to play next?" Then we'd take a request. We played "All the Small Things" by Blink-182. We even did a version of "Rolling in the Deep" by Adele. I was playing the wrong chords, it was pretty awful.

I looked terrible, too. I wore white shoes, black jeans, and a bright, white long-sleeved shirt, so I was matching my shoes with my shirt, which wasn't something I was meant to do. I looked like an idiot. I was confused.

ASHTON:

I remember that all our parents turned up to that show and they were asking questions like, "What is this?"; "Why are we at this dingy pub?"; and "What is my son doing?" It must have been weird for them.

We did four or five songs on electric guitars and then the boys did their acoustic thing. That's when I came off stage and watched them play from the back of the room. They played songs they had jammed together at school and I hadn't heard some of them before, but they sounded great. Compared to how we are now they weren't that good, but back then it was awesome.

As I stood back and watched, I could tell that Calum and Luke's voices were amazing together; Michael wasn't singing that much back then, but it was a powerful performance. I still say to this day that it was the best gig of my life so far because it just happened, even though we had barely rehearsed. But it all came together, like it was meant to be. That night was the real birth of 5SOS.

LUKE:

The 12 people who turned up to our gig were really dedicated because the Annandale Hotel was a very difficult place to get to. It was a pub and there wasn't a train station nearby, so the fans who did show up must have made a huge effort. When we finished we all went outside to meet them and say "Hi," and because everything had gone so well Calum decided that we should ask Ashton to join the band full-time. He even got down on one knee, as if he was asking him for his hand in marriage. It was pretty funny.

WHaT CAN't YOU LiVE WITHOUT ON TOUr?

CALUM:

My band – I love these guys. Apart from that, my phone. I'm absolutely addicted, which is pretty bad, I guess. I'm on it all the time. Weird thing is I'll pick it up and not really do anything with it, I'm just scrolling. People are always telling me to put my phone down. But social media played a big part in breaking us, so it's important to keep working with it and speaking to the fans.

LUKE:

Caffeine. I usually have some Red Bull before I go on stage every night, but I'm trying to cut down because I don't think it's very good for me. I've had so much of it I don't think it even affects me anymore. I'll have coffees throughout the day to keep me going – I couldn't do this without it.

MICHAEL:

My iPad. I watch box sets like *Breaking Bad* and *Game of Thrones* on it. If I find a good TV show, I'll watch it all the time. At the moment I'm on season three of *Breaking Bad* and everyone keeps saying how amazing the rest of it is. By the time this book comes out, I'll have finished it – I don't know how much better it can get, though.

ASHTON:

I need to have a skipping rope. I like to remain somewhat fit on tour and with the rope I can do lots of things. Me and the boys have got so good at training in tiny spaces. We can train anywhere. A personal trainer taught us that we could train in a one-by-one-meter box, so whenever I can, I'm keeping in shape. I'm especially working on my lower half because I only work the top half when I'm drumming.

What was crazy to me was that we had what felt like thousands of fans online, even though only 12 people turned up to our show. People were watching our covers and talking about them. Our Facebook and Twitter pages were getting hundreds of new likes and follows every day — sometimes even thousands. To play your first gig and all those people liking you online? That's just amazing. We had no idea that it would get so much bigger, so quickly.

TAKING OFF

ASHTON:

More and more people started watching us. I remember when we recorded a cover of the Wheatus song "Teenage Dirtbag"; it was the perfect tune for us. It was the sound we loved – the boys wanted to be a Green Day, Blink-182 kinda band, and "Teenage Dirtbag" allowed us to do that. Everyone was saying, "Yeah! There's four of you, you're a complete band now." And that's when the image started to come together.

What our online fans were latching onto were the four characters in the band. They were liking the personalities behind the music. I was the loud one and I was very outspoken at the time, and I was probably the most motivated in the band – I got everyone to practice, to make sure we got everything right. I could also drive, so I'd spend all my money on petrol to get everyone to rehearsals. I even snuck Calum out of school on a few occasions.

Luke was the baby, but he was the talent as well – he had the voice. Michael was the darker one – he was the punk spirit behind the band. And Calum? He was the songwriting force. He would come to rehearsal and say, "I've written this song, I don't know what it's like ..." And then he would play a brilliant riff. That's what happened with our first ever single, "Out of My Limit," which we later put on iTunes.

LUKE:

I guess it was around that time when we first got a manager. His name was Adam, and he'd tried to contact us through Facebook and our school, but he didn't have much luck. When he finally got an email to the band, he told us that he wanted to organize a tour for us all over Australia. We would be playing Sydney and Melbourne one weekend, then the next weekend we'd be playing Brisbane and Adelaide. It sounded incredible.

The plan was this: Monday to Friday we would go to school, like all the other kids, but on Saturday and Sunday we would be playing shows all over the country. I don't think our parents were too happy about it. Everyone was saying, "Oh, it'll be like the Annandale Hotel shows, nobody will turn up." But the first time we put gig tickets online, the website crashed. All the tickets were gone in five minutes. We were on the phone to each other, getting so excited, saying, "What?! How did that happen?" Those venues only held two or three hundred people, but to sell them out was such a big deal for us.

MICHAEL:

God, that tour was so weird. The first time I'd ever got on a plane was to fly to Melbourne, and I was going there to play a sold-out show to 250 people. I was only 15, so it was a pretty surreal experience. In my head, we were just little idiots, four weirdos, and it didn't make sense that all these people wanted to come and see us.

When we got to our first city, everything was so brand new. At the time we were all staying in the same hotel room. They were like apartments. We'd get this one big room and there would be four bedrooms in it. We used to

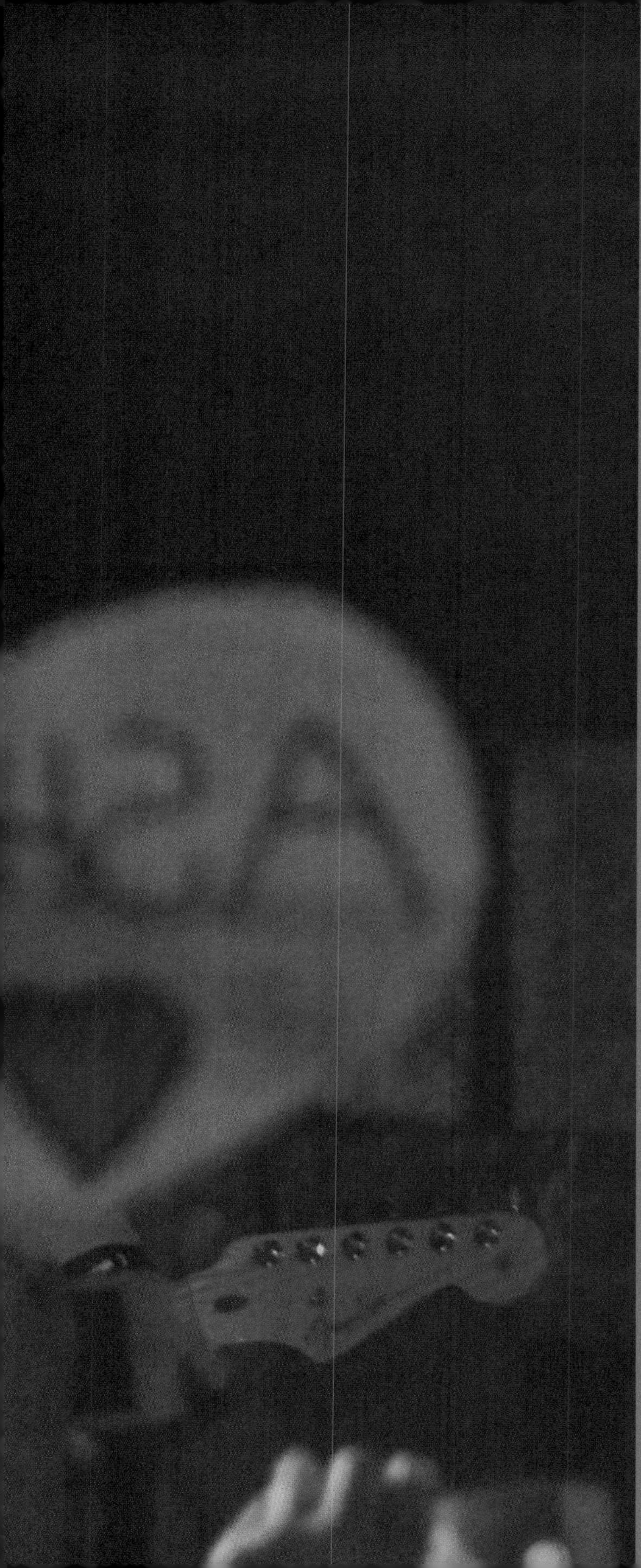

pull the four beds into one room so we could talk and joke around all night. We loved it.

As the band started to take off, my time spent at school became pretty nonexistent and I think I always tried to skip my way out of classes until I left. As I got older I thought, *OK, I have to go a bit more so I don't fail.* But I failed anyway. The day that I was allowed to legally leave, I did. I'd just turned 16 but I was having too much fun with 5SOS to care about my grades. I couldn't wait to get out.

The weirdest thing that happened to us was before a show in Melbourne. The day of the gig, our manager got a phone call saying, "The venue fell into a sink hole — the gig's off!" We were like, "What?! Wait, all these people have been waiting for so long to see us play and the venue falls into a sink hole?!"

We didn't know what to do. We thought, *Do we sit outside and play an acoustic show, or just not do it?* In the end, we had to do a last-minute venue change to a high school down the road. We didn't have any of the equipment and it was the smallest stage in the world, set up on a tennis court, but we didn't care — we were just so happy to be playing.

CALUM:

We were best friends traveling Australia, playing music to people who wanted to hear us. I think the most exciting shows for us were the ones with the smallest audiences. There was so much energy in those rooms.

At first, we were all nervous about traveling. Michael was especially nervous because it was his first time getting on a plane. We were like, "Don't worry, Michael, it might do a few loop-the-loops in the air but you'll be fine." He was completely terrified.

I guess it took a while for our parents to become completely supportive. In the beginning, we weren't playing to a lot of people and Mum thought I was just joining a band to get girl attention, but after a while they came around. They came to the gigs and got on the planes with us to make sure we were fine. Once they were used to it they were happy for us to go on our own. They became like, "You know what? This is a good thing!"

What was amazing to me was the fact that we actually had fans around the country. That was weird. We were riding around in a van to the show, all squished together and seeing people outside the venue, actually lining up to see us. It was the best feeling ever. Without them we wouldn't have been doing those shows. The fans were so special to us and it was great to meet them every time we played.

No one at our school knew we were even doing this. We were just living another life. But the worst thing was coming back to classes, because it was like coming back down to Earth. I was like, "This sucks." In Math I didn't really wanna be there. Every day I was just thinking of playing music – it's all I wanted to do. It was the same for all of us. The band was our new life.

OUT OF

PARt 3:

OUR

LIMIT

tHE
ONLY
ReASON

LUKE:

It hasn't taken me long to realize that we'd be nothing without our fans – they've been behind us all the way, from the very first minute. They've watched our videos and told all their friends about us. But most of all, they've given us the inspiration to go on. We feel like we've got an amazing, loving, passionate 5SOS family out there and they're so important to us.

It was strange at first, though; knowing that there were people all over the world who were into our music and knew everything about 5SOS, even though we were just four dudes from the middle of nowhere in Australia.

I can remember the first time I was asked for an autograph – that was weird. Me and Michael had traveled into the city on the train to do a little acoustic show. This was before our tours of Australia, so it wasn't like we were playing sold-out shows all the time. We walked across the road to eat in McDonald's when a couple of people came up to us and asked for autographs. I felt so confused because we hadn't worked out what our autographs should look like. It still is weird, but it's something we appreciate so much.

MICHAEL:

There's a loving relationship between us and our fans, and it's been there from the start. At the beginning they were getting to know us because all we had were our tweets and our random videos online. There was nothing else for them to grab on to at that time, which meant they were always excited to meet us, and that hasn't let up, though I remember the first time someone cried in front of

me. I was so shocked. I was like, "Hey, are you OK? I feel so bad you're crying."

Getting asked for autographs? Now that was a surreal experience for everyone. I didn't even have a signature when the band first started, and when somebody asked me to scribble my name down on something I had to make a signature up on the spot. It was awful, it looked like the MasterChef symbol and now I'm stuck with it and I hate the way it looks.

Posing for photos was even weirder, though. I had no idea what to do. Whenever someone asked me for a picture, I'd just stand there and stare at the camera. I must have looked pretty lame. Before, when somebody wanted a photo, like my mum, I didn't really acknowledge how to look happy for the camera. I'd just think, *Oh yeah, I'll take this photo with my mum — it's all good.* But as soon as our fans wanted photos and they were asking to take pictures with their phones, well, I had to learn how to not look stupid. I don't think I've mastered that one yet ...

ASHTON:

I thought it was strange that we even had fans. There was a time on YouTube when it was all about people doing covers and putting them online. That was when we'd just started and everyone was doing covers. If a new song came out, your band had to be the quickest to cover it and there was a constant battle to do the first version when an exciting new single came along.

Our problem was that we just weren't very good at it. We weren't punctual at all. We were disorganized and when it came to doing it, we'd do it once and think, *Yeah, that'll do. We'll put the first take up.* Still, the number of

hits and views our pages were getting started going up and up and up ...

Behind the scenes we weren't focused on covers, though. We were fixed on our live performances and how we were going to get that part of our band right. That was the important thing to us, but it was a bonus that we were getting noticed online and people were listening to our songs – even if they were covers.

It was pretty crazy to have YouTube. I remember we used to be obsessed with the comments from our fans, especially when it came to what people were thinking about us. A lot of people said we weren't very good, I guess because the covers weren't that organized – they didn't sound great. But the people who did like us were the ones that kept us going.

It felt good to have those fans because the attitude towards us at home wasn't always nice. We thought that a lot of people in our area didn't like us because we were trying to do something different. It was the four of us hoping to make something out of music and that seemed pretty sad to them.

Our parents didn't understand what we were doing (though they came around); our friends didn't understand. We were going away every weekend, touring Australia. We'd come back, go to school for five days and then we'd be hanging out until Friday afternoon when we could pack our bags and go to another state again. The only people who really understood were the four of us and our fans online.

CALUM:

It felt weird to us calling fans "fans," as we were just four dudes who were trying to start a band, but learning that we had these guys out there who liked us was really cool. When we went on tour, I was being approached by people from a city that I'd never been to before and they were wanting to hang out and get photos and stuff.

I remember, a year after the band had started to take off, me and Ashton spent Christmas in Edinburgh, in Scotland, because I had some family there. We were just walking down the street and this girl came up to me and was like, "Can I have a photo?" We both looked at each other. I knew we were both thinking the same thing: *What?! Someone in Edinburgh wants a photo? That's so strange.* But it was brilliant as well, and we knew we were very lucky to have those people supporting us.

LUKE:

It was Good Charlotte's *The Young and the Hopeless*. It was so cool, even the title was amazing. I remember when I was little I made my mum drive me to the shop so I could get an album and I picked this, even though I didn't really know who they were at the time. Once I played it, I thought it was the best album ever.

Because none of my friends at school were really into that kind of music, they all thought I was a bit weird – especially as I had the long hair. I also remember the artwork was great – there was a picture of the band on the back and they all looked really punk. That's still one of my favorite albums today.

CALUM:

I was on the school bus one day, it was really early in the morning, and my sister's friend's brother came up to me and gave me a burned CD. I looked down and it had "Green Day – *American Idiot*" written on it in permanent marker.

I put it in my s**tty CD player and I was instantly in love with it. Green Day was the reason I picked up an instrument, fell in love with songwriting, and wanted to be someone in music. The second track, "Jesus of Suburbia," blew me away. It was about 10 minutes long, but it was so amazing to think that someone could actually write all those different parts in one song and make them all equally good.

MICHAEL:

I think it was Eminem's *Encore*. I went through weird phases in my life where I wanted to be a rapper, or be an amazing guitarist. I've also wanted to be a video-game designer. I've probably been through everything!

Eminem was definitely one of my stages – at the time I loved everything about him. In the beginning when he was first coming up with stuff like this, I could rap every lyric of his songs – as embarrassing as that is to admit now!

ASHTON:

Mine was Jet's *Get Born*. We play their single "Are You Going to Be My Girl" before we go on stage. They were an Australian band and I got into them because I loved rock. I used to watch TV every day, waiting for live performances to come on because there was something I loved about watching a band live. Jet were always on at the time and they were great.

the first album i got was...

WE'VE WORKED TOO HARD FOR THIS JUST TO GIVE IT UP NOW

LUKE:

We headlined two different Australian tours during 2012 and around that time we signed a publishing deal with the record label Sony ATV. After that we spent our whole time rehearsing, because we knew things were getting serious. We'd come home from school and rehearse. Sometimes we'd skip school too and just hope our parents didn't find out. It was fun times.

In the end we got a rehearsal room, so we could practice properly, as it was becoming a real drag having to share a mic at Michael's garage. The only problem was, our parents had to pay for it because we didn't have any money. In the end we got this room, but it was a pretty s**tty place! There were three mics and a PA, and the place was very small and smelled real bad.

We rehearsed so much that we even played in the dark some nights. I'm not sure where the idea came from, but our thinking was, *If you can play without seeing each other or what you're playing, then that'll make things harder ... and it'll make us a better band!* I'd like to think it worked out all right.

That rehearsal room was very important to our band. We were practicing five times a week because that's all we wanted to do. We were desperate to be a great live band like the acts we loved growing up – Good Charlotte, Jet, and those guys. I remember us playing the songs over and over and over so we could really tear it up when we got on stage.

After that, we were asked to open for a band called Hot Chelle Rae in October 2012. They had become a big deal in Australia and were about to appear in much larger venues than we'd been used to. I'm talking shows where 2,000 would pay to get in – and that was a huge step up for us. Luckily, because of all the rehearsals in our crappy little room, we'd started to sound way better live.

One time, while we were jamming at home, I remember all of us looking at each other and thinking, *We're a proper band now – this is working.* The music sounded good and we were playing tight. The thing is, we probably weren't even that good, but at least we felt good playing as a band together.

IN A SMALL WEST SYDNEY TOWN, ONE TEENAGE DRUMMER CYCLES 10KM TO AUDITION FOR 5SOS...

...ARRIVING AWKWARDLY SWEATY.

HEY GUYS I MADE IT

ERM, OKAY.

COOL?

BUT YAY – NOW THERE'S A BAND!

THE DAY OF THE FIRST GIG...

ANNANDALE HOTEL

OK, SO ONLY 12 FANS SHOW UP – WHO CARES?!...

5SOS ARE BORN!

✴ MMM , MILKSHAKES ✴

manager

ONE DIRECTION tour dates

AT THAT MOMENT , SSOS' MANAGER TURNS UP WITH SOME CRAZY NEWS

ONE DIRECTION WANT SSOS TO SUPPORT THEM ON TOUR ! TIME TO PACK UP AND MOVE TO LONDON.

5sos Video brainstorm

HOW TO MAKE THE "DON'T STOP" VIDEO THE BEST EVER...

SUPER HEROES

BAGSY RED!

I GOT BLUE!

YES! BLACK!

ERM, GREEN, I GUESS?

(IT'S ALRIGHT, CAL, FLUORESCENT GREEN IS SO YOUR COLOR)

5SOS: SUPERBAND TO THE RESCUE!

CAL PAL

CALUM:

The big thing for this band was to be one of the best live acts around. The bands that we loved were incredible when they played gigs, we could see that from watching them on TV or playing their live albums at home. We wanted to be as powerful as Foo Fighters or as energetic as Green Day. And we really worked hard at it. We sucked at the start, and at the time we were supporting Hot Chelle Rae, we only had a few songs of our own, like "Gotta Get Out" and the others that I'd written in my bedroom. But me and Luke were writing some new songs. They were coming together in an organic way and we knew we had it in us to make more music, better music.

LET'S GET OUT

LUKE:

We recorded the *Unplugged* EP in between the two
Australian headline tours. I remember we had to get a lift
from my mum into central Sydney, which is a couple of
hours from where we live. It was a big day for us and a
bit of a road trip. We recorded it all that day but I
remember feeling pretty sick at the end of it; my voice
had gone and I wasn't able to sing very well, but we still
got it all done. We recorded "Gotta Get Out," "Too Late,"
a song by All Time Low called "Jasey Rae," and a cover of
the Blink-182 hit "I Miss You."

What was great was that we had made a little bit of
money from our tours over Australia, and when we put it
together there was enough for us to cover the cost of
recording. That felt really special.

CALUM:

We'd never properly recorded anything before, especially
not in a real studio. We were pretty nervous about it! But
it was great laying down our songs in there. There was
loads of stuff we could fool around with and we were able
to play really loud. We were curious about everything
and how it all worked. It was such a proper laugh doing
it, too.

LUKE:

After that, the single got to Number 3 on the iTunes chart, and to be honest, I didn't really know what that meant. I'd never been on the iTunes chart before, but I knew it was a big deal, even though I didn't really appreciate just how big at first.

Then the single went into the Top 10 in Sweden, but all I could think was, *Why? How do we have fans in Sweden? How does that happen?* I remember that our manager at the time, Adam, got us together as a group to tell us the news of our small success and we were so confused by it all. We were just four dudes from a school out in the sticks in Australia.

CALUM:

By then, we were all very committed to the band. We had to grow up a lot to be able to make the decision to say to our families, "The band is what I want to do from now on." Our parents were sketchy about it. Naturally, my mum was like, "What future are you gonna have? You could go to university and get a real job." But I was like, "No, Mum, I'm doing this."

AND THEN...

MICHAEL:

I'll never forget the moment we were told that we'd be
going on tour with One Direction. We were in Adelaide
on our third Australian tour, sitting in a diner booth,
drinking milkshakes, when someone – our manager at the
time, I guess (that's how blurry it was) – put a piece of
paper in front of us. When I looked down it had all the
One Direction dates on it. Everyone was scared half
to death.

What?!!

We were told: "Louis Tomlinson has found you guys …
One Direction are looking for a support for next year …
They want you!"

It was a pretty mental thing to happen out of the blue
like that. We were all silent for about five minutes and we
didn't know what to think. When I looked at the number
of shows and the size of the arenas we'd be performing
in, I knew we'd be playing to around one-and-a-half
million people in total. Up to that point we'd only done a
few shows and the biggest gig we'd played was to 2,000.
Everyone was stunned.

The band had a big talk about whether it was going
to be the right move for us. Of course the numbers were
great, but were 5SOS going to be seen as a boy band if
we did those shows? That was the thing. After all,
supporting One Direction was about the most pop

move we could make. Were people going to judge us
for that?

All those questions came up because we knew that
One Direction had a different style to us. Don't get me
wrong, we loved them; their songs are ridiculously good
and they had managed to revive the whole boy band
scene when they first started up. But what we didn't want
was for people to say we were the next One Direction,
mainly because our sound was totally different.

It didn't take long for us to figure out that being called
all that stuff wouldn't matter in the long run. After all,
we'd be getting our music out there to hundreds of
thousands – millions – of people. It would be up to us to
change people's perception of 5SOS. We knew it might
take a long time for One Direction fans to realize that we
weren't a boy band and that we had punk and rock
influences. But we also worked out that it would be so
worth it to play that tour and we will always be very
grateful to the boys for the opportunity we had.

I remember a few months down the line when we were
writing some new songs with Benji and Joel Madden from
Good Charlotte, they were telling us that they'd started
when the boy bands *NSYNC and the Backstreet Boys
were still huge. For some reason everybody thought that
Good Charlotte were a pop band, too, even though they
were nothing like one, but if you look now, everyone who
talks about Good Charlotte sees them as a legendary rock
act. We wanted to be leaders like them and bring guitars
back to the radio.

CALUM:

While we were sitting there, shocked, I turned the pages of the tour schedule and it was just endless arenas around the UK and Ireland. All I could see were pages of dates, names of the cities we'd be playing: London, Glasgow, Cardiff, Dublin, Manchester, Sheffield, Liverpool ... I was like, *S**t, there are so many cities and so many shows!*

We'd never thought of playing arenas before. I don't think it had even crossed our minds that we could do it, so to get the news that we could be supporting One Direction was a shock. It came out of nowhere. We'd gone from playing in front of 2,000 people in clubs in Australia to performing for 18,000 people a night in cities on the other side of the world. It was an amazing opportunity for us and we couldn't thank the One Direction lads enough.

OUT OF OUR LIMIT

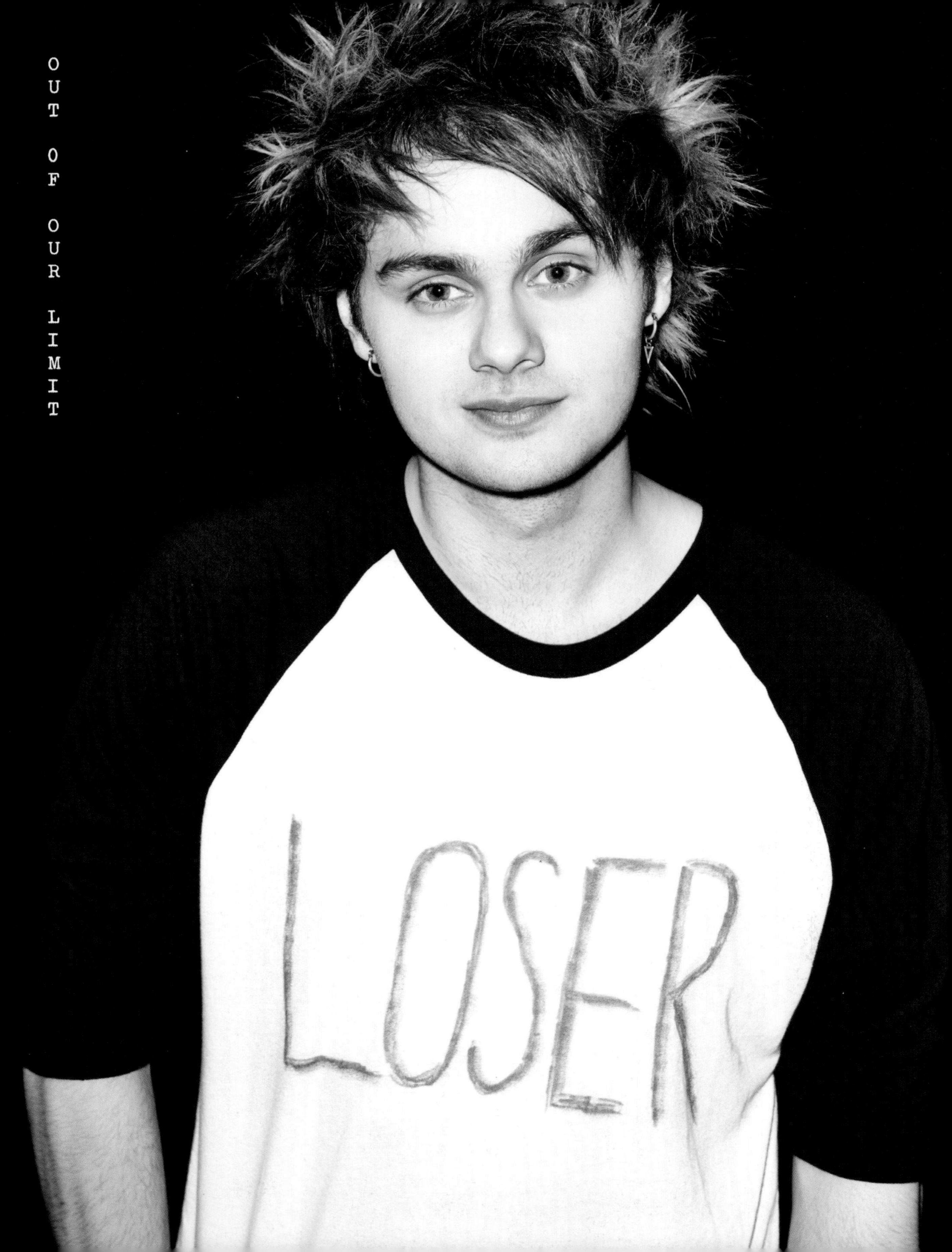

CALUM:

As soon as we got the news, we knew we had to get serious. We got a new management team called Modest! and they figured it would be good for us as a band to move to London so we could write with some great songwriters they knew. With a little help we'd be able to put together some new tracks and learn how to play those huge venues.

That was a big step, a massive step. We worked out that we would have to leave our families for nine months, and that wasn't easy, especially for us. I think we were all around 16 years old except Ashton, who was 17, nearly 18. It was a massive move for us as people, but we were all really excited by it. We all wanted to write some good music, and we knew it was the right move for 5SOS.

MICHAEL:

To tell your parents that you're leaving to go overseas at the age of 16 was hard enough, but then to say that you didn't know when you were coming back, and all of it was to be in a band? That was seriously tough. I remember my parents were sad about it, but they were always so supportive of us, and while it was probably hard for them in the first few months we were away, they understood why we had to do it.

It was hard for us, too. We'd been so used to a life of waking up every day and hearing our parents talking downstairs. We lived normal lives; we had a routine where we would go to school all week and then go to band practice. On the weekends we would play guitars as much as we could before starting it all over again on Monday morning.

Suddenly, everything was about to change. We would be living in a random house in a city we had never been to before — or at least not spent a long period of time in. A few months earlier, we had been taken to London to meet Modest!, who were based there, but staying in a city for a few days wasn't the same as moving there for nearly a whole year.

The good news was that we were all best mates and we would be together. But the thought of having to adjust to a brand new country was scary. We'd have to get the Tube to different places, and get black taxis to drive us around London. That was pretty fun but also intimidating, but it was what we knew we wanted to do if we were to become the best band that we could be.

ASHTON:

I had just finished school forever, and three days afterwards I was moving to London for nearly a year. That was pretty exciting, but upsetting at the same time. I had to break up with my girlfriend and I had to say bye to my mum and my family. Me and the boys were going on an adventure! It was a new beginning.

I remember the flight because it was the first time I had seen Michael cry. He hadn't really been anywhere in the world outside of Australia. I'd traveled a little bit, the other guys had traveled a little bit, but Michael hadn't experienced that much life until the band came along. He was leaving everything he was used to, and it must have been tough for him.

I remember giving him a hug and saying, "It's alright, man. It's going to be good." I sat next to him for the journey, trying to cheer him up.

CALUM:

We were in Melbourne playing with 1D. I'd bought these jeans the day before and as I spread my legs, the denim ripped from the knee to my crotch. I looked around to see if anyone had noticed and quickly pulled my knees together. Then I signaled over to our guitar tech, mouthing the words, "My jeans have ripped."

He came up to the stage and when we were playing "Teenage Dream," the lights went down. I snuck off stage and he taped me up while I started playing. He was sticking me together while I was playing the bass lines backstage! But when I came back out, it hadn't worked. My jeans fell apart again and I had to announce it to the entire arena. It was awful.

LUKE:

One time, we left a venue in Sweden, ran to our car – which was surrounded by fans – and drove for 10 minutes out of town. When we got to the hotel and looked out of our bedroom windows, there were loads of girls arriving. I was like, "How did that even happen? How did they get here so quick?" To be on the other side of the world and have people actually like our music was amazeballs.

ASHTON:

When we were in LA, a French horn band was sent to our house. We had some fans hanging around outside and they were like, "How can we come hang out with you?" I told them, "If you order us a French horn band you can." It really was just a joke. About an hour later, I was watching *The Simpsons* on the TV and I thought, *Can I hear a brass band?* When I looked outside there were four guys with their instruments, playing on the side of the street.

MICHAEL:

Oh god, this is so bad: we were walking down the road with some fans recently and I was trying to take a picture with this girl. As I was holding the phone, I accidentally tripped her up. I don't know how it happened. She fell and I was like, "Oh my god, what have I done?! I'm so sorry! Are you OK?" She shouted, "I think I broke my foot!" Luckily she was fine, but that was a pretty awful experience.

WHAT'S YOUR
FUNNIEST OR MOST
MEMORABLE MOMENT
FROM TOURING?

LONDON CALLING

MICHAEL:

What a shock. When we landed there, it was right in the middle of winter. This was January 2013, and it was the worst weather they'd had in years and years. The temperature was freezing cold.

I think the first day we got there, it snowed. I was used to the sun and hot weather in Australia, and that was the first time I'd ever seen real snow. When I woke up in the morning I walked downstairs, but before I could even get to the door, Calum, Luke, and Ashton were already running outside in their underwear. It was ridiculous.

The house we had in London was so much fun. I want to go back there one day because there are so many funny memories from those days. We were four dudes, away from our parents, and every day we'd sit down and play *Call of Duty* and *FIFA* on the computer for hours. We'd run riot around the house. It was great to be living together.

CALUM:

But then the hard work started. For the whole time that we were in London, we wrote pretty much every day with lots of different songwriters, and it was pretty full on at times, especially as it was all a new experience for us. By the end of a day we were all braindead. We couldn't really think – not that we cared. Writing songs was so much fun, especially when you love who you're writing with. Then it's not like work at all, it's just hanging out with your mates writing songs.

ASHTON:

We would go out and write songs every day. We had five months until the One Direction tour started at the O2, so we needed more tracks than the ones Calum had written in his bedroom. So, with the help of some great songwriters, we went into an intense period of getting tracks down. We were probably writing 12 a week, so it was kinda full on. I'd go into a studio with Michael to write a song, and then the other two boys would go and write another song the same day somewhere else. So we'd be writing two songs a day. Man, it was tough. They were long days, but we knew it was going to be so worth it.

MICHAEL:

We worked with James from Busted, we worked with the guys from McFly, we worked with Nick from Kaiser Chiefs, Scouting For Girls ... We worked with so many people, just to see who we could create the best songs with, and also to become better songwriters ourselves. That was always our thing: we wanted to write our own songs just like Billie Joe Armstrong, Kurt Cobain, and the Madden brothers had done – the artists we grew up with.

Lyrically we were writing about things that we knew about, subjects that were important to us while we were in London, or had been when we'd been growing up in Australia. Me and Luke even wrote a song called "18" — the story behind that was the fact that, at the time, we were really bummed out about not being 18! We couldn't do this or do that. We wanted to go out so bad, but Ashton was the only one who was 18.

There were some other tracks I love too, like "English Love Affair" and "Voodoo Doll." The cool thing is, even after all this time we still play those tracks now. We wrote for a long time but eventually we felt ready for the One Direction tour.

ASHTON:

We all wanted to be in the biggest band in the world and we were prepared to work hard for it. I remember when the weather got better, we decided to rock up to Hyde Park, which was in the middle of the city, and do a random little performance. There's a Hyde Park in Sydney too and we'd once played an acoustic gig there, so we figured, "Why not do the same thing in London?"

The first time we showed up, 30 people came along. Then we did another and 70 people arrived to see us play. It wasn't a lot, but we were thousands of miles away from home and we were building a little British fan base and making the most of our opportunities, because me and the boys wanted it to work out so bad.

Our only problem then was that we had major confidence issues as a band. That came from the fact that we were brought up with the Australian mentality. At home you didn't talk about yourself, you didn't talk yourself up. You weren't encouraged to be loud about yourself, or to be a character.

PUT IT
AWAY

5SOS
BIRTHDAYS

JANUARY 25th 1996
Calum's birthday

JULY 7th 1994
Ashton's birthday

JULY 16th 1996
Luke's birthday

NOVEMBER 20th 1995
Michael's birthday

But to be in a band that wanted to conquer the world you had to be louder than life, you had to be a character. We didn't like that. We felt a bit awkward talking to people. We sucked in interviews when people wanted to find out who we were and what we were up to. I remember I was the only one who really talked when people asked us questions. The other boys would be silent. Michael might have said something every now and then, but Calum and Luke would say nothing.

Looking back at that time in London, we were a band on hyperdrive. We were learning how to work on level terms with all these other bands that were huge in the UK. It was a whole new world for us, and we worked so hard to get everything right.

HIDING OUT IN A DREAM

ASHTON:

When it came to playing those shows with One Direction, the venues were crazy. When we first set out on the tour, we were going to do 10 shows at the 02 Arena in London. Then we started playing it twice a day, every day – in the end we played 10 days there. All in all we played something like 115 shows across the UK, Ireland, Australia, New Zealand, Canada, and the US, and that's when we learned to be a band and discovered our sound. Today, if we were to play a smaller venue – to 2,000 people maybe – we would hopefully blow the roof off, but it wouldn't have happened without those shows. We learned so much.

The size of the shows freaked me out at first, but we all handled it differently. The thing is, I wanted to be better. On stage I wanted to be Billie Joe Armstrong from Green Day, or Dave Grohl from Foo Fighters. My problem was that I was behind the drums and there aren't many drummers out there who will talk to the audience and sing. Playing arena shows was new to all four of us, so the others were in the same boat. We had to learn how to be great in big venues and rock amazing shows.

CALUM:

I don't think you can ever feel prepared before playing in front of 18,000 people for the first time. We had a week or so of rehearsals and we all felt relatively ready until we saw the size of the first arena in London. We all looked at each other and went, "What?! I'm not sure what's going to happen tonight."

We went on stage and played our set and everyone seemed to go crazy. We'll never know who was the most nervous but I reckon it was me. I was definitely trying to hide it, but it probably wasn't working. People I saw afterwards said I looked pretty nervous, but looking back it's still mental; it was the O2 Arena and I'd probably c**p my pants if I played it now.

All I can remember is that it was absolutely crazy having 18,000 girls screaming back at us. At that time I was full of adrenaline, I couldn't really hear anything and I wasn't really thinking. The show was so big and exciting. It was a bit of a blur – it still is.

MICHAEL:

Funny, I watched the video of our first show the other day and I could see the very first things we were doing when we walked out on stage. I looked at my face in the video and I seemed so scared, I'm pretty sure I was actually shaking. It was that intense.

After a while, I started slowly walking from spot to spot, just standing in front of my mic, not looking happy – in fact, I looked miserable. In my mind I know I was thinking, *This is f***ing cool!* But back then we didn't know how to convey our feelings to the crowd.

The part that I'll always remember from that first night was when we started playing a song called "Over and Over." Just before the guitars kicked in, we asked everyone to get the lights up on their mobile phones and the whole arena just lit up. I don't know how we got everyone to do it, but it seemed like every person in the crowd was holding their phone in the air. Just to look out on that sea of beams was amazing because every one represented a different person. And those lights went back as far as I could see.

CALUM:

After a few gigs we stopped being nervous and the shows became more exciting. We were thinking about how we could improve the performance and the tour started to become more and more fun.

It helped that the One Direction guys were really genuine. They were really supportive. I remember coming off stage one night when I was really disappointed with my playing, and Louis was standing there. He could tell I was annoyed.

"You know what, man," he said. "You will have those days. You're on and off for a night, but then tomorrow will be better."

As a kid on an arena tour for the first time, I really looked up to them. They guided us a lot during those early shows, which was so good; I guess we were very lucky to get bits of advice like that. But we also watched how hard they were working. Every night they would try to meet as many fans as they could, and they treated the people around them really well. It was just so nice to see that the biggest band in the world was made up of genuine, caring people.

We started to become friends, too. We could tell that they were very busy, and we were very busy, but whenever we could, we would hang out. I know there was a lot of fruit thrown around in the dressing room some nights. The music would go on backstage and there would be some heavy air guitar as well. It was all good fun.

CALUM:

We all knew that we had a lot more work to do. We also knew that we needed to make a great record if we were to fully take advantage of the opportunity we had had on this tour. It had been a crazy time for our band, something we'll never forget, but it was still about to get even crazier ... next stop was America, and that was going to be huge.

ANOTHER
AND I'M
SOMEWHE

PaRT 4:

DAY

5SOS

ERE NEW

MICHAEL:

America was crazier than we'd ever imagined it could be. We were going there as support for One Direction on their tour, but we stayed in Miami to relax for a couple of days. When we landed, we walked into the airport where we thought some fans might be waiting for us, but there was no one there. I was like, "Oh, that's cool, it's getting kinda late. Why would we have fans in Miami anyway?" Then we walked downstairs into the arrival lobby and about 150 people were waiting for us.

It was the first time we'd been mobbed. We were being pushed and pulled. We were surrounded. We couldn't move. It freaked me out a bit, but at the same time it was awesome we had fans waiting to see us.

I guess our arrival must have seemed more exciting for our American fans because it was the first time they'd seen us in the flesh. They'd been waiting a long time for us to play out there, so they were pretty stoked. It was a really intense experience, though. I was so overwhelmed because we couldn't move in the crowd. It was scary, really scary, but at the same time, we loved it. We couldn't believe so many people had come out to see us.

ASHTON:

America was the best for us because that's where most of our musical influences came from – like the towns where Good Charlotte and Green Day started up. To do gigs in the venues where those bands first played was a great thing for us. It was a real learning curve, and I think America liked us. They're really into guitars over there so it's a nice environment in which our music can grow.

CALUM:

By that stage on the tour we'd become really good friends with the One Direction lads. The first time I met them was when we were in London. We were all really young back then and when they talked together we were like, "What?!" We couldn't understand the accents, we didn't get the jokes. But it was probably the same for them.

It didn't take us long to realize that they're genuine lads. Whenever we had some downtime on that UK tour, which was rare, we'd hang out together. One time we played football with them, but they absolutely pummeled us. We were really unfit and after halftime we were like, "No, we can't do this, let's quit." We were beaten something like 10–4. Louis was probably the best one out of them – he's a decent player.

Another time we went paintballing. It was in this random place in the countryside and it was pouring with rain. The mud was intense. As we were running around, they had this thing called The Predator – some dude who dressed up as The Predator from the movies. It was the scariest thing ever. He would jump out from the trees. If you saw him you weren't allowed to move otherwise he'd shoot you. That was fun times.

One night, at the end of One Direction's UK tour, they pulled all of us up on stage so we could do a human pyramid in front of the crowd. I was like, *Holy s**t! This is nerve-racking.* I had been backstage, hanging out in my thongs [sandals] and jeans and then we randomly got this call to go up. When we got up there, I was on the bottom and I was finding it really hard to keep my balance. I didn't want to be the one who caused the whole thing to collapse. I was like, "Don't fall over!" Somehow, we pulled it off.

ASHTON:

When we got to the US, the tour bus started to smell pretty bad after a while. We had one that was built to look like a 50s tour bus and Metallica had been on it before us. They'd left all their stuff in the cupboards, like their coffee and Twizzlers. We were living off the groceries they didn't want!

We love being on a tour bus, but sometimes the schedule would get really stressful. We weren't really used to working so hard – the only pressure we'd had previously was getting out of bed in time to get to school and I reckon we even made that look like hard work! I had a part-time job at a video shop and that's not tough compared to working from 8am every day till midnight – that's a regular day for us now. But the bus felt like a little home on wheels. Even if we had a hotel to stay in, we preferred to sleep on the tour bus.

ANOTHER DAY AND I'M SOMEWHERE NEW

MICHAEL:

We get pretty close on tour. Luke even admitted to me once that he'd steal our underwear when he hadn't got any clean ones left. He'd just go into our rooms and take it. Dude, clean your underwear!

CALUM:

I remember the police threatened us in Dallas because they wouldn't let us meet the fans after the show. We were like, "We're gonna meet them." But they didn't look too pleased. One of the cops said, "Hey, you're not. And if you do, we're gonna arrest you!" We backed down pretty quickly after that.

LUKE:

Our live shows were getting really tight. We were progressing. We'd come off stage and straightaway we'd be talking about the things that we were doing wrong, or the things that we thought went well. We'd be like, "How can we make this better?" We wanted to make our live show as good as it could be.

We were a much better band at the start of the US tour — by then we knew how to work the crowd. We had only done 16 shows before playing the O2 in London, so it was a pretty intense ride, but we were trying to be a force, we wanted to show confidence and instead of being shy we had to own the stage. We had to be in charge.

You kinda have to be a little bit cocky during shows and we found that hard at first. Since those early gigs, I think we've learned to involve the crowd. We move around a lot more. We didn't do it much back when we started, but suddenly we'd become more exciting to watch. Michael was all over the place. Running around the stage was his way of keeping fit, I think.

MICHAEL:

I went from standing still on stage to running around like a lunatic. That's confidence, dude. When I watched videos of our early performances I was a little bit shocked. In my mind, I'd been going pretty crazy, but when I watched myself back it just looked as if I was walking around — especially on the One Direction shows. I realized I had to imagine what the people at the back were seeing. I had to make everything bigger. We all got that. We were growing up fast and our stagecraft was starting to get better and better.

SOME KINDA HOLIDAY

LUKE:

When we first heard we were going to be recording our album *5 Seconds of Summer* in LA last September, we couldn't believe it. We were a small band. I know we had fans around the world, but that was nothing compared to some of the bands we loved like Green Day or Blink-182. It was insane.

Then we were told we'd be staying in a big house in the Hollywood Hills and we were freaked. When we got there, I'd never seen a place like it before. It was huge! The building was glass-fronted and had a pool and amazing views of the city. There was even a studio out the back where we could write and record. We wrote a lot of the album there. It was a cool place to hang out and party, too.

Waking up every day knowing we were in LA making our first record – that was really cool. We'd written quite a few songs in London, but I think LA was where we really found the 5SOS sound.

MICHAEL:

I think that was the most amazing month of my life. When we walked into the house for the first time, I remember saying to our manager, "Are we in the right place? Are we actually staying here?" The first thing I did was run upstairs and claim the best bedroom! We recorded a lot of songs while we were there — "Kiss Me Kiss Me," "Don't Stop," "Everything I Didn't Say," "She Looks So Perfect" ...

ASHTON:

We hooked up with the legend of punk, record producer John Feldmann, and everything just clicked. He got who we were. In the UK everyone seemed a bit confused about us because there was no one else around who had our pop-punk sound anymore.

John got what we did. He liked it. He knew it was about the guitars and there was a little bit of an attitude behind it, too. John had written with heavy metal bands — the heaviest of the heavy — and he makes rock music that does well on radio, too. He'd also worked with Good Charlotte, who we love.

When John was asked to work with us, he didn't look online. He went to see us live, and when he came backstage he said, "You guys are a band. You're a rock band." We were like, "Finally! Someone's understood what we are." We were lucky to meet him.

CALUM:

We recorded some cool songs in LA. I love "Disconnected." We wrote that with Alex Gaskarth of All Time Low, who came over to work with us towards the end of the writing process. We decided to do something different and "Disconnected" became more of a drum and bass kinda song. It's a bit slower and really melodic, and I love the lyrics. It's one of my favorites.

LUKE:

Michael and Ashton had written our first proper single, "She Looks So Perfect," but Michael hated the song at first. I remember he came back from the writing session and was like, "It was really bad today. The song wasn't very good." I was like, "Don't worry, man, I've been there, I've definitely had those days."

MICHAEL:

I didn't like it at first. When I was in session with Ashton and the writer, Jake Sinclair, I was sitting there thinking, *I just don't like this song, I don't think we'll use it. I don't think anyone else is going to like it.*

ASHTON:

Jake came up with the idea because his girlfriend used to wear his T-shirt around the house. He thought there was something quite sweet and romantic about it. Then he changed the lyric to include the line "American Apparel underwear," because it was quirky. I don't think Michael was too sure about that. He said, "Well, we'll have to bail on the underwear line." I was like, "No, mate, you can't do that – that's the winning thing."

LUKE:

They came back to play it at the house, and when I heard it I was like, "You're f***ing kidding me – this is great!" It was just Ashton singing on it at that point. Everyone in the band was saying, "This is definitely a cool song." Michael came around in the end. Once we'd finished it in LA to how we liked it, we were all pretty excited about it.

CALUM:

Being in the studio was so much fun. I remember having my 18th birthday there and all the lads sent me into the recording booth. They were saying, "Sing this line, sing that line." I wasn't sure what was going on. I was like, "I don't even sing this bit." Then someone said, "Yeah, well, actually ... we got you a stripper. Happy birthday!" It was proper funny, I was like, *WTF?!*

Another time, we were in the house one night when Michael came up to me a little freaked out. He said, "Someone's trying to get into the house!" I looked out and I could see people shining flashlights through the windows.

I was terrified. We went to the upstairs window and we could see these guys. But I remember thinking, *Why are they wearing such tight pants?* Eventually, they went away, but the next day some fans were hanging around outside. They were like, "Oh, we got you some male strippers last night as a surprise." Through all of that chaos, it's amazing we even managed to finish *5 Seconds of Summer*!

I'm so proud of the album, though. It took us two years to write, but what's really cool is that one of the songs, "Beside You," is one of the first we ever wrote. It's great that it's survived. This is going to sound weird, but we're my favorite band — we write the music that I love.

LONG WAY HOME

LUKE:

It was time to go home. We'd been away from Australia for nearly a year, but the One Direction tour was rolling that way and we couldn't wait to get back to see our families. It had been such a long time that we'd been away. It was weird going from that to my bedroom in Western Sydney with the old posters on the wall.

There was such a different attitude to our band in Australia, especially at that point. We hadn't done anything there for a while and it felt a bit like there was some negativity towards us. I guess that's because we hadn't released a full record there yet and we'd been away for so long. The response has been a lot better recently, though, which I'm happy about because we love where we're from and all our fans there.

The first thing I did when I got back was catch up with my family and our dog, Molly. I loved being at home, doing nothing. It was nice to do normal things. Of course it was a great experience doing all those crazy things with the band — making music, living in LA, touring the world — but it was so nice to have some normality, and see family and friends, to bring us back to Earth. In a sense it all still felt a bit surreal when I was away from home.

Before too long we were back playing shows. This time it felt extra special as we had grown so much as a band and now we were back home doing gigs. We had our families down and they could see now that our band was a real thing. It felt as if we were proving to them that what we were doing was real. They hadn't seen anything of us for ages because we'd been overseas. Hopefully they were proud and could see now that all our time spent rehearsing and saying we wanted to be in a band was worth it.

It was really nerve-racking, though. I get the most nervous playing in front of my family — even now. I think it's my brothers that make it quite tough. They're builders and carpenters, and they're quite manly — they have manly jobs. They must think what I'm doing is pretty weird.

CALUM:

The crowds were great in Sydney and throughout Australia. I was home for about a week and it was surreal. On tour I usually wake up and check my schedule first thing. I know I'm doing this, this, and this. When I went home I was like, "What do I do now?" I just hung out with the family and it felt so cool. My mum makes the best spaghetti.

The funny thing was, after a day at home I was bored so I called Ashton. I should have been sick of him. I should have been sick of all those guys, but I wasn't. I'm not sure why. I guess it's a sign that we're all such good friends.

MICHAEL:

The first time my parents saw me perform at a proper show was at the Allphones Arena in Sydney doing the One Direction thing. They'd been to loads of concerts there — like the Stones and stuff — so I felt really proud because now I was playing there! It was amazing. It was the first time they'd seen me in a year and it was great to see them dancing along to our music.

It's weird how you can feel the same whenever you go home, no matter how long you've been away for. We had two days off, and I just stayed in the house, had dinner with my parents, and went to sleep. That's exactly what I was doing before I left. I hope stuff like that doesn't change. I always feel it's the younger me when I go home. It's definitely comforting being in those surroundings when you've been away for so long.

I think before we went away home seemed really boring. It sucked. But now home is the best. I appreciate it so much more.

ASHTON:

I was really worried that my grandparents wouldn't like the music when they came to see us. The whole time I was thinking, *Oh, I'd better not swear on stage!* But in the end it was the same as when they came to their first 5SOS show, which had 200 people in the audience. They were blown away then; and they were blown away again.

It was insane the way things had elevated. Two-and-a-half years previously we'd been in Michael's garage with tins of paint everywhere. It was dirty, we had dusty drums and a few amps the size of a cardboard box, which sounded like crap. Then we went on to rock the Allphones Arena in Sydney. Pretty crazy for us four dudes.

TURN THE RADIO LOUD

MICHAEL:

We were looking for our first single, and we needed it to be a "moment" because it was our first proper release. We wanted to blow people away. We had a meeting where we talked about potential songs and singles, and there was a moment when one of the boys said, "Let's go with 'She Looks So Perfect' as the first single!" Everyone started nodding: "Do we wanna do it?" We all looked at each other and said, "Done! First single."

LUKE:

It didn't seem real, to be honest. I think it was nice to have something out finally — to have something that acted as a statement for us as a band. Honestly, I would have put out anything at that point because we had spent so long on all the touring, writing, and building the band.

When "She Looks So Perfect" was released there were people at home I knew who were texting me. They were saying they'd heard our record in a club, or a shopping mall. It's funny, we'd supported One Direction on a whole arena tour and did all those headline shows but nobody outside our close friends said anything about it. Then when they saw us on TV they were like, "Oh ... my ... god!"

WHAT'S YOUR FAVORITE 5SOS MOMENT SO FAR?

CALUM:

The first show we played at the Annandale Hotel was one of the best moments. Actually it was one of the best and the worst because the gig was so bad, but I remember a lot about it: getting down on one knee and saying to Ashton, "Will you join the band?" It was the first time we took group photos, too. We looked f***ing terrible, but it felt like something special.

LUKE:

When we went to Number 1 in the UK. That was a special moment. You can't really beat that. We topped the charts in only a few places – Australia, Ireland, NZ – that week, but that felt like a proper event. We were in the UK at the time and I thought it was such an achievement for an Australian band. It was a big statement for us. We went into a radio station to celebrate. Then we flew to Sweden that night to do five shows in five cities. That was tough. We had to get up at five every day, but we had to go out at night to celebrate, too, so we'd go to bed at three and be up at five to do it all over again. It was pretty intense, but extremely worth it.

MICHAEL:

The album coming out. I was so excited for that day, when all our family could listen to it and all our fans could have it in their hands. It was the best moment. I knew it was going to be the best moment months before, because it had been such a long time in coming. We'd been making the album even before we went on the first One Direction tour in 2013.

It's always been about trying to make an album for us. There are songs on there like "Beside You" that were written two years ago.

Hopefully it's changed people's perception of us, so they can see we're a proper band.

ASHTON:

My favorite moment is repetitive: it's sitting behind the drums and looking out into a sea of people. It's my favorite view of the world and it happens every day when we're on tour.

That's been the best thing so far; there's nothing better than looking out at that. It's why I don't get to sleep very easily on those nights. It's impossible to come down after that madness.

ASHTON:

As soon as the song was released, we were looking at the charts all week. We'd heard it could be Number 1 in the midweeks and we felt lucky our fans were behind us. They really wanted us to get the Number 1 spot that week. They were awesome.

MICHAEL:

Duke Dumont was in the mix for Number 1 as well and every day we'd be saying, "How many has Duke Dumont sold?" We were constantly thinking, *Are we still in the mix?* We pushed it so hard but we wanted people to want the record because they liked it, not because we had tweeted saying, "Go get it!" if you know what I mean. I even heard "She Looks So Perfect" in Starbucks, and I was thinking, *I'm in Starbucks getting a coffee and no one here knows that I'm the guy singing all those "Heys!"*

ASHTON:

The day of the news was like Christmas morning. Everyone woke up and I went in to see the boys. We were all looking on our phones for any news. We were scrolling down on Twitter and everyone was saying, "Oh you're Number 1 in the UK!" All of us were desperate to tweet the news, but we held off until we had the proper confirmation. You never know sometimes ...

Not long afterwards we got an official email that said, "Number 1 in the UK!" But then the other figures came through as well. We were Number 1 in other places, too. We were like, "What the hell's going on?"

CALUM:

I think it went to Number 1 in Australia first because the charts work differently there. I hope we proved ourselves by doing that, though I don't think Mum got it. I'm not sure if she realized what it meant. It really hit home with us, though. I remember looking at the lads and thinking, *Wow!* There were many bro hugs at that moment!

To know that people wanted to buy our music was so, so good, especially for a band coming from where we do. We're just four dudes from Western Sydney. We were just kids. Outsiders. Pop—punk fans. It was really humbling that people actually liked our song.

ASHTON:

The first time I ever heard the song from an outside perspective — not a writer's perspective — was when it came on the radio shortly after it had got to Number 1. It was strange to hear it up against other songs. We were in a car and it came on Capital Radio. It made it seem more real to hear it with a DJ talking over the beginning and the end.

CALUM:

I was at a club in Australia when the song came on. I was having a night out with the crew and they said, "Let's go to a club." I was like, "OK, yeah!" I was sitting there minding my own business, having a drink, and I just heard the opening chord of "She Looks So Perfect" and I thought, *What?!* I looked around and all the crew were laughing. I thought, *This is the best moment of my life.*

ASHTON:

Having the Number 1 made us feel like we belonged. We were always playing our songs at shows to people that didn't know our music. Our fans were listening to our songs online, but most of them had been recorded live. They didn't know any of the new stuff but they rocked out anyway. To have the single out and to have it go to Number 1; to know people had heard it and they could scream the lyrics at the top of their lungs ... that was a big moment for us. Dude, it was huge.

HOW DID WE END UP HERE?

ASHTON:

We wanted our videos to be unique. We really looked up to what the Foo Fighters and Blink-182 had done on their promos – which was comedy. I think that's what gets people into a band's personality. We always have a laugh doing what we do, and if people can laugh along too, then that's good.

We decided we really wanted to make funny videos and we wanted people to look forward to them being released. We didn't want to be doing what everyone else was doing. Our videos had to be different, otherwise we wouldn't put them out there. The ideas had to be new. They had to intrigue and challenge people.

MICHAEL:

We had so much fun making the video for "She Looks So Perfect." It was the first big-budget thing we'd ever done. Before then there were a couple of videos, but they had been very low-key indie productions. When we did "She Looks So Perfect" there were film crews, massive cameras – it was all a bit crazy.

When we started filming we could tell the video was going to be really good. It was exciting. It was awesome.

The concept was so us. It was as if the director had been drunk in the ideas meeting and had announced, "I know what we'll do! We'll put the cameras here ... and theeeeen everyone takessssh their clothessssh off!"

CALUM:

I remember walking onto the set of the "She Looks So Perfect" video and thinking, *Whoah, this is actually happening?!* When it got to the point where people were ripping off their clothes I had to stay focused because there were like half-naked people everywhere. It was tough to concentrate for the day!

Then we had to take our pants down and the video went all fuzzy. We liked to keep the fans guessing about what was going on with our underwear. I think and hope the fans liked it. Maybe there'll be a director's cut with the full pants-down scene? I definitely would have stuffed some socks down there! And I had some embarrassing underwear with animals that should probably stay covered!

LUKE:

By that time we knew how to perform, so we could bring a lot of energy to the camera in our live performances. It was in-your-face kinda playing. I think that really made that video. But with all the people there — the crew, catering, the extras — it was a bit like being a movie star.

MICHAEL:

When we got the idea for the "Don't Stop" video – us dressed as superheroes – we were so excited. Who doesn't want to do a video as a superhero? I don't know of any band that's done a video where they've made superhero alter egos. It was a cool idea.

I think because we're so different individually and each of us has his own distinct personality, the alter egos really gave our fans something more to hold onto. That's all we've ever wanted to do: to make our fans feel close to us. Our fans know we're complete dorks. It was good for them to see it in a video.

A couple of days before the shoot we had to try out all the costumes. It was really hard to get the stuff we wanted. We were all stuck with the colors. I walked in and took red. Well, I had red hair at that time, so I had to be red! Ashton chose blue because he loves blue and Luke was already wearing a black outfit, so that was the closest shade he could wear. And Calum was left with green! The only suits left were either lime green or purple, so he didn't have much luck, but I think he looked cool in lime green.

Making that video was so much fun. We filmed it in LA, on the same spot where some of the scenes from *The Dark Knight* were filmed. First we did the scene where Luke chases the ninjas. We were sitting there watching it with the director and I was like, "I wish we were making a longer-length film, I wish this wasn't only three minutes ..."

CALUM:

We were living out our childhood dreams filming the video for "Don't Stop." It was so much fun. I was the really flamboyant lime-green dude — Cal-Pal. I didn't have a special power in the video, but I had a stunt man, which was just as exciting!

LUKE:

That costume didn't smell that great after two days, but the video came out so well. I was a little bit worried it would come out too kiddie, but it rocked. I was Dr. Fluke. I was going to be Dr. Luke but there was an issue — well, the real Dr. Luke dude might have had an issue with it — so I had to change the name slightly. It was a good time. At the end we were on the rooftop in our superhero costumes. That looked awesome on film.

MICHAEL:

I'd spend my whole life in a superhero costume if it was socially acceptable. That was the most fun video to shoot ... so far.

CALUM:

Not long after that we played the Billboard Awards in LA. That was really nerve-racking. The audience was full of stars. Pete Wentz from Fall Out Boy was there — it was cool knowing we were playing for him. But there were other people in front of us, too, like Nicki Minaj. It was really scary for me because of the musicians in the audience, but it was fun to do.

We had to wait behind a curtain before our performance and that was the scariest five minutes ever. I was looking around at the lads and we were all so nervous. It was mental. It still wasn't as nerve-racking as playing those assembly shows at school, though. When we came off stage we were absolutely buzzing, but we had to leave straight after, so we didn't get to hang out with anyone, which sucked a bit – instead we got on a plane!

MICHAEL:

When we were first told that we'd be playing the Billboard Awards, I was like, "What's that?" Then I was told, "Oh, you know the one where this person played and that person played." I thought, *Oh my god! I watched that. Holy balls!* On the day I asked one of our crew how many people watched the ceremony on TV. He gave me a look and said, "Are you sure you want to know?" I thought about it for a second and said, "No, don't tell me."

The performance was amazing. It was the first really big TV we'd ever done. There were rehearsals with cameras, and that meant we had to perform in the soundcheck in the same way that we were going to perform on the live take. That way the cameras could capture it all. That was weird. Pop videos feel very different because you know you're making a small movie, so it kinda feels like you're performing. Plus you know that loads of people will be watching the videos. With the soundcheck it's different. But the final performance was damn exciting.

Man, it's so weird: the band had taken over all our lives. At that point, I couldn't even remember a time when I wasn't in the band. Every time I tried to think about it, it was gone. Like the memories had been wiped from my mind!

LUKE:

It was all exciting. But I think the thing we were buzzing about was the release of the album, *5 Seconds of Summer*. We had recorded so many great songs in LA. We were really looking forward to the record coming out — we were very proud of the tracks.

There was the song "Good Girls," which was written in London but recorded in America. Me and Calum went to the writing session with Roy Stride from the band Scouting For Girls. During the first day he came to us with some ideas and he said, "What do you think of the lyric, 'Good girls are bad girls that haven't been caught?'" We were like, "Nah — that isn't really us." But Michael loved it — well, it's more of a Michael thing — and when he and Ashton worked on the song it came out great and our fans absolutely love it.

"Kiss Me Kiss Me" was one of the first songs we did with John Feldmann in LA. Alex Gaskarth helped us to write it. That was strange because we all knew everything about him. We were very fangirly around Alex, because he's in one of our favorite bands — All Time Low. He's really nice, really chilled out. He's just a band guy, I guess. There was no ego. All Time Low were really supportive of us. A lot of people in that scene were a bit unsure of us at first, but Alex really helped us. He said, "Hey, these guys are cool."

ASHTON:

Life didn't really change in a click-of-the-fingers type of way once the videos were out and the album was finished. I think me and the band have never rested on our laurels. We've always been like, "OK, what's next?" We've never thought, "OK, we can take a rest now." That's just not us.

We've never been content with what's happened. We played Wembley Stadium earlier this year, supporting One Direction, but one day we dream of playing there as headliners ourselves. That would be incredible. When I go out and play I wanna absolutely dominate it. I want the security to go, "That guy is a great drummer." I want the mums to think, *He's amazing!* I really wanna be one of the best drummers in the world one day. I don't know when I'll be able to say that – I don't know if I ever will be able to – but I want to give it a shot at least.

The fans have given us the chance to be recognized for doing something we love. To be recognized for playing the drums is so cool for me, because it's what I've done all my life. When I wasn't at school that's all I'd do. Now people care about it and that's really nice. No one gives a crap when you're playing in your bedroom, everyone wants you to shut up. Playing through a big-ass PA to 80,000 people or even 20 people, it doesn't get any better. It's sweaty, noisy fun ... with a lot of chicken afterwards. We do love a Nando's! Luke definitely eats the most – he has long-ass legs.

It's the same thing with our first album, *5 Seconds of Summer*. I want everyone to love it, not just our fans. I want the girls" dads to listen to it and think, "This is all right, I can get into this." I really look up to bands that got everyone on board, like Green Day. Everyone liked them. I want us to be the band that everyone gets. I don't want us to be stuck down.

DReAM DAtE?

CALUM:

Will Smith – a real man crush. I think he's so cool. Seriously, though, it's always Katy Perry. Every girl answer is Katy Perry. What a human being! I feel like she'd have a good story to tell, especially about how she got into music. I love how she's hard-working and passionate about what she does.

LUKE:

Jennifer Lawrence would be good. She'd be nice. I'm not sure where we would go because she's quite a big deal. Where do you take a girl like that? You'd have to go somewhere really impressive. I think dinner's too clichéd. Maybe we could go see one of her movies? Actually, that's pretty lame. It would have to be dinner.

MICHAEL:

Me, my laptop, and ice cream!

ASHTON:

I don't think I've found the person to be my dream date yet. I'm not the kinda guy who wants to date celebrities. I think that's pretty lame. If you're genuinely in love, then cool, but there are lots of other lovely people out there, too!

THE

PART 5:

FANS

I. CALUM:

We've got the most dedicated fans in the world and in the past two years I've realized that our fans are the best thing that's happened to this band. They were with us from the very first YouTube video, the very first show. Even though our fan base in Australia was quite small in the early days, those guys were so dedicated. They traveled all over to see us and meet us. They bought tickets to all our gigs.

I remember some of the first Australian tours we played – that was wild. We were selling out venues that held 200, 500, sometimes even 1000 people and it was amazing to see that people knew the lyrics to our songs. I'd be standing there thinking, *Damn, I wrote that song in my bedroom and now there are hundreds of people singing it back at me? That's insane!* When I used to play in those days, I'd be jumping up and down with excitement at the realization. I was so stoked.

Our fans are that dedicated all over the world, though. When we supported One Direction in the UK and America, it was cool to see 5SOS fans getting their seats. When the shows arrived, people were wearing our T-shirts. The fact that people were coming to see us as well as One Direction gave us a lot of confidence and a lot of belief in what we were doing.

In the UK the fans would hang around outside our hotel all day. They would jump on the minivan when we traveled to the venues. But it's the same all over. They're equally dedicated in the rest of Europe as they are in America and Australia. I remember we went to Europe for a week and when we played in Spain people were singing outside our hotel. We'd never experienced that before. It was a different atmosphere, something we'd only dreamed about.

Italy was cool as well. To think that people liked us over there was just so weird. I mean, we didn't speak any Italian. Well, we come from Australia, we live so far away from anything else, there's no point learning another language! We sang in English, so it didn't seem real — I'm not sure they even understand us! But we loved it there. The food was insane, it was the best I'd ever tasted on the road, but it wasn't as good as my mum's spaghetti!

And then there's all the presents. Chocolate, candy, all the gifts our fans give to us — so much stuff and we're thankful for all of it. The sweets do kill me at points because I have to stay fit, but the most important thing is that we have a connection with those fans. When people want to meet us and talk to us — we'll do it. I hope that never stops happening.

Like most bands, we get asked for autographs all the time, and I admit that, yeah, it was a little weird at first. I was like, "You want me to sign something? Really?!" But now it's so cool and we appreciate all the attention. That's why whenever someone wants to take a picture with us, we'll always stop and hang out where we can. We've realized that maybe one day people might not want to follow us around the world, so we want to appreciate every minute with them that they want to spend with us.

Sometimes bands forget that the fans are the most important thing. Not us. If ours hadn't helped us in the beginning, we wouldn't be doing this. Seriously, without you guys we'd still be in Western Sydney, hanging out in Michael's garage, playing songs to nobody. Luckily, their support got us here. That's why they're the best in the world. And that's why we love them.

2. LUKE:

We can go anywhere in the world and our fans will be there for us. Man, it's so cool.

From the start they've been so dedicated — and not just in Australia. We can get off a plane anywhere in the UK — somewhere like Newcastle, Manchester, or London — and there will be people there waiting for us. At first that seemed weird, but now it's become the normal thing. It's great to see them getting excited when we arrive.

One thing I can't work out is, how do they know where we are? Fans at one airport must figure out where we're going and then tell the fans where we're flying to. When we touch down they're there waiting at Arrivals to say hey. It's so cool, though.

We'll also get to a hotel, check in, and by the time we're ready to go to our rooms, five minutes later, they'll be there. At first it'll be just four or five people, but an hour later there'll be 200 hanging out. But that's always amazing to see. The fans do so much for us and that's why we're able to do what we do — write songs, make albums, and play shows.

Seriously, we wouldn't be where we are without them. They got us attention at the beginning, when we were still making YouTube videos and playing small gigs around Australia. That got us started. If no one had been interested in our music back then, no record label would have wanted to sign us. But that cool fan base got us attention.

Now it's spread around the planet – to the UK, America, Canada, Sweden, Mexico, all over. It's crazy in Italy and Spain, too. We did five European countries in five days to celebrate the release of "She Looks So Perfect" earlier this year. It was tiring, getting up at 5 am, flying somewhere, doing interviews, playing shows, and then falling into bed around 3 am for two hours' sleep before doing it all over again. But the fans kept us going.

The first place we went to was Sweden. Then we went to Germany, France, Italy, Spain ... It was tough at first and a little disorienting. We didn't speak any of the languages – and the people who couldn't speak any English were very confused when they met us.

I remember we got chased down the street in some parts of Europe. It was so funny – we'd seen it happen to other bands, but we never imagined it would happen to us. We got chased in America and in England on a small scale, but in mainland Europe it was on a whole other level.

In Italy and Spain we'd try to get to a venue in a random car and the fans would surround us. Then when we'd get out it would look like a scene from one of those zombie apocalypse shows like *The Walking Dead* – just hundreds of people running towards us. *AAAAAAAAAGHHHHHH!*

When we first started 5SOS, one of the early gigs we did had 500 people there and that was cool for us because there were all these heavier bands saying, "Ah, 5 Seconds of Summer sucks." Later we'd play small festivals and there would be a band on one stage and we'd be on the opposite stage, but we had a load of fans watching us, so that was pretty cool.

Earlier this year, we went back to Australia to tour and there was a girl who came to our Sydney show who had been at our first ever gig — one of the 12 at the Annandale! And she was following us still. I thought that was amazing. It showed how much she cared.

It's only been two-and-a-half years since we played that first show, but it's been a long two-and-a-half years. Plus, our performance was pretty terrible that night. But that girl must have seen something in us. For her to stick around all that time was really cool. It's people like that who have got us to where we are today.

CALUM:

There are too many, but I think it's gotta be Green Day for me. Billie Joe Armstrong, Tre Cool, Mike Dirnt – they're the ultimate band. I was watching a DVD of their stadium shows recently and the way they control the crowd is just amazing. Everyone's in the palm of Billie Joe's hand.

LUKE:

Billie Joe of Green Day. I watch him all the time on YouTube. I don't think I'd even want to meet him because I'd probably freak out. He's a great frontman, he's very smart, but I also think he's underrated. To be able to lead a stadium like he does ... I dunno how he does it. I aspire to do that.

MICHAEL:

Spiderman – he's the s**t! I think he shows that anybody can be a hero, even a mild-mannered photographer, a weird guy who doesn't know anything about anything. As far as music goes, though, it has to be Alex Gaskarth from All Time Low. He's the reason I got into singing and playing the guitar in the first place. He's the best ever.

ASHTON:

Dave Grohl. He's conquered the world with his music and vision, and I really look up to that. I'd love to do some guitar and sing like he does. Who knows? I'm different from other drummers because I talk to the audience a lot. I'm very loud to the crowd. I'm the rock'n'roll voice at the back of the band.

My grandpa is my hero, too. I've never had a dad, but he's sort of been my dad. He's a very wise guy. He taught me that it's OK to be human sometimes. I put a lot of pressure on myself when I was younger to take care of my brother and sister when times were tough with Mum. He told me that it was OK to be upset about it, to feel things and not be a brick wall all the time.

WHO'S YOUR BIGGEST HERO?

3. MICHAEL:

It's been so nice to be able to give our fans the album. There have been some people who've been waiting two or three years for it. Now they can finally have a piece of us. Yeah, they can get a T-shirt, or an EP, or a single, but it's not the same as an actual album.

For the past year, when people have said to us, "When can I get a record?" we've always answered, "Soon!" That's all we've been able to say for two years. "Soon ... Soon ... Soon!" Now when people ask us we can say, 'It's out!' Not soon. Now. The fans can physically get it. It's so exciting.

There are some fans who've been with us from the very beginning. One girl in Australia, called Melissa, has been with us since before our first gig. I saw her when we went back just a couple of weeks ago and was like, "You've been a fan of this band longer than Ashton has been with us ... and you're still supporting us? That's really nice."

She's awesome – all of our fans are – but it's weird to think that some of them have watched us grow from those first videos to the shows at Wembley Stadium. It must be so amazing to do that. I wish I could do that with a band – to see them blossom and develop into something big.

Without these people, there's no hope for our band. If there are no supporters, there's no band. That's how it goes, and we couldn't be where we are without the people who have been supporting us. If people didn't come to the shows there'd be no tour. If people didn't buy records, there'd be no more recording sessions, so everything revolves around other people. Like I say – no supporters, no band.

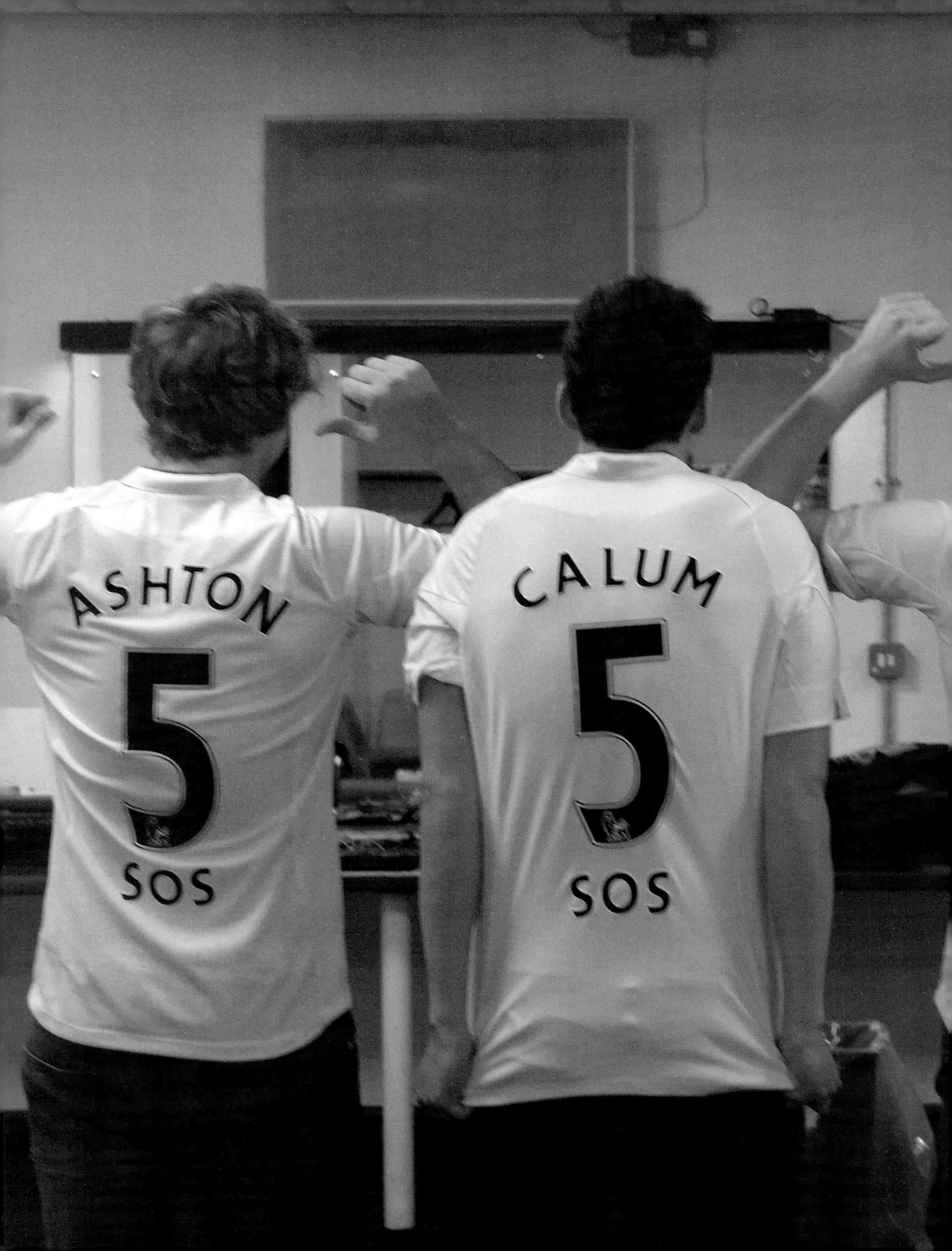
ASHTON
5
SOS
CALUM
5
SOS

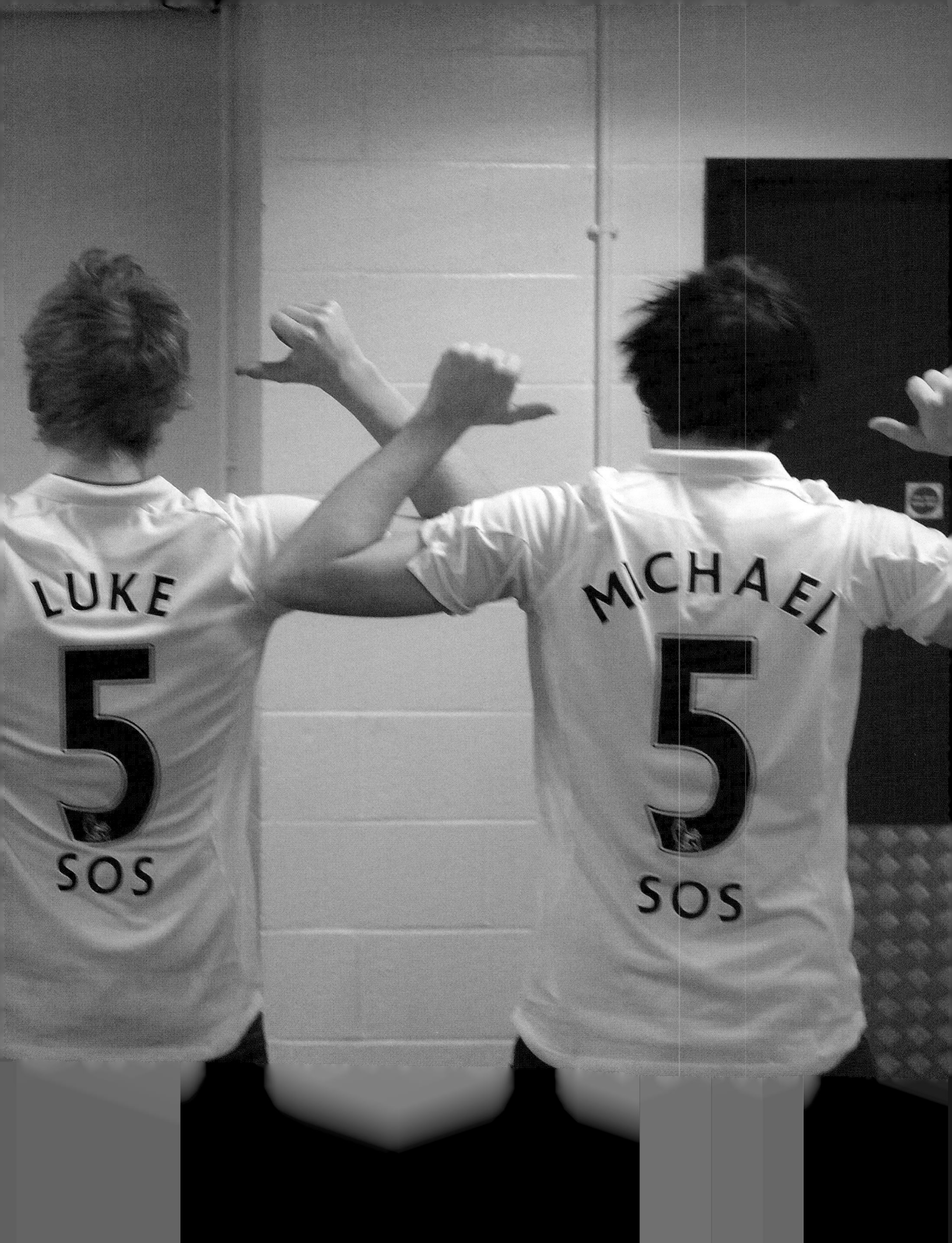
LUKE
5
SOS
MICHAEL
5
SOS

It's mad to travel the world and have the fans waiting outside our hotel on the other side of the planet, though. It's the perfect reminder that we're doing something good. We always say that it's weird that people want to meet us. Even when we're in Milan or New York, they'll be hanging around the radio stations or wherever we're doing promo or shows.

When that happens, I always think, *Those fans are here to see us? But I'm not that special.* The fact that all those people have become pumped for four stupid dudes ... it's weird! But it's so nice at the same time. It gives us a sense of reassurance that we're doing the right thing. We want to keep making those people happy for as long as we can.

When things go crazy, when the fans are waiting for us and hanging out, I feel really humble. We all do. If there's ever a mental moment where a hundred people chase us down the street to our hotel, we always get inside and look at each other, but without ever really wanting to talk about it. We're shy.

The last thing we want to do in this band is give each other egos. We'll never be like that. If someone starts being a dick in 5SOS, we'll tell them they're being a dick. We've been like that from the start and it's really helped us. For us to be as close as we are and still feel like we're the same four guys ... that's been good.

If one of us says anything lame or incredibly douchey, they get cut down by the others pretty quickly. We like to take the p**s. Like if Ashton wears a stupid hat he's going to get stick. He can't pull off a Pharrell!

But it's our fans who have made us this way. They're the ones who really keep us grounded. We can't thank them enough.

IT'S YOUR LAST MEAL EARTH: W ARE YOU ORDERING

CALUM:

For the starter I'm going to have a chicken and corn soup, with bread. I'm a soft-roll kinda guy, with a bit of butter. For the main course I'm ordering a Sunday roast – I'm going for lamb, Yorkshire puddings on the side, with loads of veggies like carrots, peas, some green beans. I like to keep it simple. Then I'll pour plenty of gravy over the top. I don't like my gravy either thick or thin – somewhere in the middle.

I always feel bad when I eat desserts, but as this is my last meal on Earth I'll take a hot chocolate brownie with ice cream! Then I'll wash all of that down with a good lager.

?

LUKE:

For the starter, I'll take the red pepper dip from Nando's. Nando's is *so* good, I love it there. I was thinking about having a Nando's for my main, but I'd still like to be quite healthy. Recently I've been really into my chicken schnitzel with gravy and chips. As for dessert I'd love to have cookies-and-cream ice cream — I'm really into that. I'll have a pint of lager to go with it!

MICHAEL:

I'd like some poppadoms to start. No matter what the main was, I'd order a big plate of the stuff — 100 per cent. And without the dips, too. I've eaten four bowls of them at an Indian restaurant before.

I think I would go for a fillet steak for my main, with chips. I like it cooked medium rare and with a Jack Daniel's sauce on top — that's a BBQ sauce but it has whiskey in it. For dessert, I'd have a warm chocolate brownie with ice cream melted on top. I've been hunting for the perfect brownie for a long time now. Oh, and I'd order a beer to go with it.

ASHTON:

Garlic bread, first up. Then Mum's spaghetti — I used to look forward to it all the time. I never used to eat at school, I would wait until I got home. If Mum had cooked spaghetti it was always in a massive bowl and it was the best thing ever. For dessert you can't beat an ice-cream cake. There's a Cadbury's one that is great. It's what you'd probably give to a four-year-old for their birthday, but I don't care. To finish off I'll have a Pepsi. No beer for me.

4. ASHTON:

Every band is going to say this, but our fans are everything to us. The thing is, I don't think they genuinely understand what they've done for 5SOS. In the place we're from, people thought we were so weird. No one gave a crap about us or our music and we couldn't wait to leave. It makes me emotional just talking about it.

We'd get cut down. People talked down to us. We didn't have any other friends, we were outsiders. It was just us four and we were stuck there. People in our school thought we were oddballs because we were playing in a band and writing songs. We just wanted to leave so bad, but the fans were kinda like the Hand of God. They picked us up and got us the hell outta there.

I hope that can inspire other people – whatever it is they're doing – to persist with what they want to do. Self-belief and the support of other people can get you to where you want to go. Look at us: times were tough, man, especially with our families. There was no money and it was rough – really rough, sometimes. But thanks to those fans who had a belief in us two-and-a-half years ago, we're here now, having released our first album, and playing shows in America, Europe, Australia ... everywhere!

When we see the fans, it's so cool. There are lots of them, but we like to think of all those people as individuals who see something in our band. It's great to think that people really care about our band. And if we can make them happy and do what the band does to make them feel something special, then that's the best.

Of course it blows my mind. I used to see what we're going through now on the news, but it was about other bands. I would sit there and go, "How the hell did they do that? Why are people acting like that with this band?"

DESCRIBE YOURSELF IN A FEW WORDS

CALUM:

Hairless: I just don't have any hair. I don't have any on my legs, my arms ... it doesn't grow! All the other guys give me stick for it.

Shy: My mum told me recently, "When you were younger, doing your football trials, me and your dad said, 'For every person you go up to and say, "Hello, my name is Calum," we'll give you $2.50.' " Apparently I only made $2.50. I didn't want to talk to anyone.

Clumsy: Sometimes my brain switches off and I go into cruise mode, and then that turns into accidents. And ...

Party Tech: Everyone needs someone to bring the party together!

LUKE:

Strange: I'm a bit of a weird dude. I think you have to be a little bit insane to do this. I thought I was really uncool at school, too, so I'll also say uncool.

Legs: I'm 60 percent legs – everyone says I have really long legs, really girly legs. We're all quite tall in 5SOS. It's weird, I worried that we wouldn't be successful because we're so tall and a lot of my favorite artists are pretty small – Billie Joe of Green Day, Kurt Cobain was small, Pete Wentz, too ...

MICHAEL:

Hungry: I'm always eating. I'm a pretty avid eater. Food is great.

Foxy: I don't know why – I just like foxes, I guess.

Sleepy: I love my bed, I love sleeping. I spend as much time as possible trying to sleep because I think that's how you become a better person.

Geeky: I'm still a computer geek – I have games on my laptop and I take it everywhere. I'll play a game for a couple of days and then I get bored with it.

Weird: I think we're all probably very weird. We're strange people. I think Calum is the weirdest. He tries to act like he's the most normal, but he is definitely the weirdest. Ashton tries to hide it too, but he's weird as well. Me and Luke are fine about showing that we're weird.

ASHTON:

Loud: I like to yell and sing at the top of my lungs and I have a lot of issues when we're in hotel rooms. The people next door always complain.

Moody: I have big mood swings for some reason. I can be happy and loud, even jumping around the room sometimes. Other times I'll be very quiet and just want to listen to music. That's just the human I am.

Forgetful: I'm terrible at remembering most things.

Rock: I'm a free person. Rock is about a lot more than music to me. It's about being comfortable with the person you are and hopefully being loud about it and spreading that attitude to other people. It's OK to be different and an individual.

Active: I used to be a swimmer, but I still like to keep fit with Calum. That's our bonding thing. To play the drums as best I can, I have to be fit.

We love playing Australia. There's a sense of belonging. The fans there know that they were the beginning of things for us, especially in Sydney. It's not as fanatic as it is everywhere else in the world, and I guess people maybe think it would be, but I guess the attitude is: "Ah, there are those guys who come from an hour away on the bus."

I think that's why the people from where we're from find it weird. People who know us from home say, "You guys are just those dorks from Western Sydney." They don't understand that when we go to Mexico, or Sweden, or Spain, it's a huge deal.

It's a weird thing for them, like it is for us. I don't expect them to understand. When I try to explain our life and the band's fans to my family, it's hard. When they say, "What have you been doing?" I'm like, "Aw, the usual, just playing shows." It's really hard to explain what the life is like.

It's always odd going home, though. It's a different world down there – from a music perspective, too. It's not the same as anywhere else. Australia feels a bit like it's in its own little bubble. I guess it's so far away from anything else. But when we saw our fans there, having been away for so many months, the reaction was as ridiculous as it had been anywhere else.

The thing is, there were police at the airport and I just hated it all. I hated all the fuss. I wanted to see the fans and look at them and say hey, but the police were holding them back. They were separating us. What was really weird was that when we flew out a week later there was the same amount of fans at the airport to see us, but there were no police. It was just the fans. It was great. I much preferred it the second time.

The one thing I do find crazy is when people get tattoos of the band. And it's wild that they spend all their wages on traveling around to see us because it makes them happy. But I'm glad that they do. And I love that they live by the lyrics we've written, in the way that I've done with my favorite bands. I'm just knocked out by the whole thing, really.

As soon as we had the Number 1 with "She Looks So Perfect," everyone went crazy, but we only got there because of our fans. I'd hate to think that we'd be a band that went to Number 1 and then stopped meeting our fans, or forgot to pay respect to the people who got us to where we are.

I hate it when bands think they've done all the work and don't have to meet anyone or wave to anyone. I don't want us to be that band. I want to give our fans much more. When I get on stage I think, *These are my drums, this is my band.* And we know what we're doing, we're just gonna give the people out there everything we've got.

I don't get nervous. I know how to play drums better than anything else I can do, and the stage is my office — that's what I do. Instead of feeling nervous, I go on stage and think about how I can get our fans to have one of the best nights of their lives. When I go off stage I want to be able to hear the crowd scream.

I want them to want more.

We all do. They're everything to us.

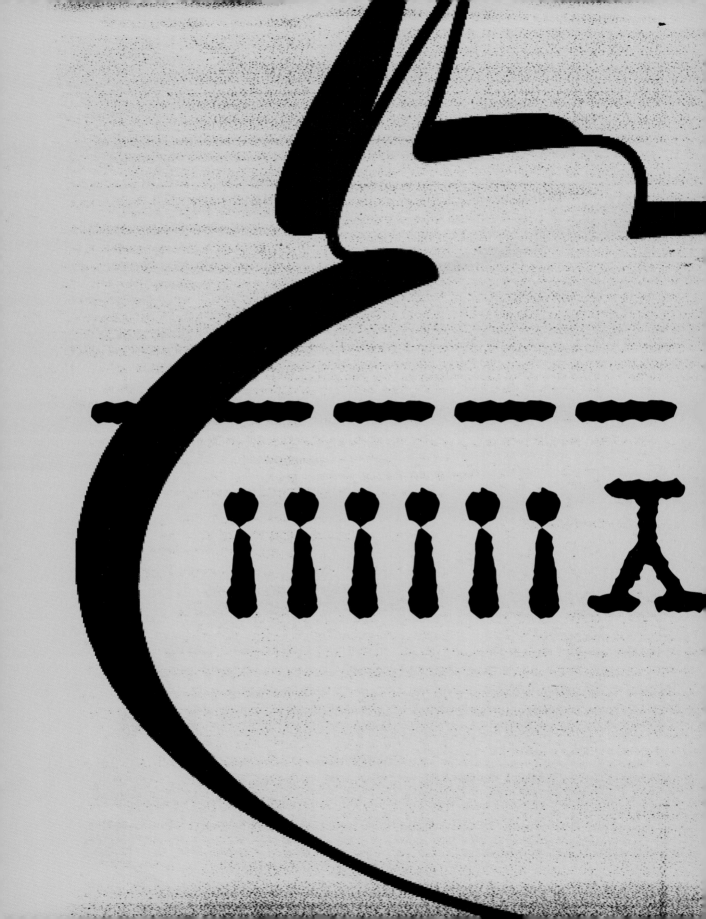

G'DA